END

Joe Campolo Jr has compiled a wonderful collection of his words and thoughts in this collection called "On War, Fishing & Philosophy." Already a fine novelist, Joe's observations and anecdotes cover a wide range of subjects, from war to fishing in Wisconsin lakes. It is a fun read.

>   Tom Keating, Author, "Yesterday's Soldier"

I enjoyed all of the articles, and bits of philosophy in "On War, Fishing & Philosophy." Joe writes about serving in the Vietnam War, his articles are very interesting, yet not bitter. Joe also covers other life events, where he shares more philosophy, and a good bit of humor. I thank Joe for this book.

>   Rick Wehler, Author of the Minne-Sconsin book series

Joe's latest book features a nice bunch of stories that we can all relate to. I very much enjoyed reading "On War Fishing & Philosophy" as it brought back many memories for me.

>   Peter Beining, USAF Vietnam War Veteran

I really enjoyed "On War, Fishing & Philosophy," a book of short stories and philosophical thought by Joe Campolo Jr. It is icing on the cake for The Kansas NCO trilogy. Entertaining, insightful and a fun read!

>   Ted Kmiec, Partner at Kmiec and Noonan, LLC

Joe Campolo Jr

On War, Fishing & Philosophy

Copyright © 2021 Joe Campolo, Jr.

All Rights Reserved. No part of this book may be reproduced or transmitted in any form or by any means, electronic or mechanical, including photocopying, recording, or by an information storage and retrieval system (except by a reviewer who may quote brief passages in a review to be printed in a magazine, newspaper or on the Internet) without permission in writing from the publisher.

This a book of non-fiction—all the stories illustrate individual reactions to actual events. Some names have been changed for privacy reasons.

Library of Congress Control Number: 2021941032

ISBN: 978-1-943267-82-8 Hard Cover

ISBN: 978-1-943267-83-5 Soft Cover

Edited by Joyce Faulkner

Original Artwork by Trieu Hai Hoang

Printed in the United States.

This book is dedicated to those who graciously shared their stories for our reading pleasure.

And to my family and friends, who encouraged me to write.

And to my readers, who have supported this wonderful journey in writing.

And to Red Engine Press, who made it all possible.

Table of Contents

Introduction	ix
Section I - *War and the Military	1
Section II - *Outdoor Recreation & Activities	112
Section III - *Work & Life	145
Section IV- *Guest Writers	164
Section V - *Philosophical quotes from Joe & Others	194
Closing - Sweet Bird of Youth, by Joe Campolo Jr.	242
Authorizations	244

Introduction

The Kansas NCO trilogy, by Joe Campolo Jr, has been getting great reviews ever since the books were published. Joe created a website, www.namwarstory.com, to showcase his books and keep readers appraised of his activities. His website also features various veterans' causes and activities.

Joe's website blog features many stories about his time in Vietnam, and the military. The blog also contains many of his hunting and fishing adventures, and some other life stories as well. While some of the stories in Joe's blog are sobering, many are lighthearted pokes at some of the misadventures Joe has experienced in his lifetime. Many of these stories are included in this book. Joe's blog features many guest writers, and some of their stories are included in this book as well.

Joe's curiosity and observant nature has inspired his own philosophical quotes. Those, and quotes of others that Joe admires are also in this book.

Many of Joe's blog articles have appeared in various magazine and newspaper publications.

Sit back and enjoy *On War, Fishing & Philosophy*, Joe's latest book.

Section 1

WAR AND MILITARY STORIES

These stories are the result of my four years in the military, including one year in Vietnam during the war. Those four years, and particularly that one made an indelible impression on me.

I hope you enjoy them.

Memoirs and Essays of the Vietnam War
Introduction

In war, everybody loses. Participants sacrifice their lives, limbs and sanity, perpetrators their morality.

Joe

The Vietnam War Memorial in Washington D.C., a wall of healing.

This section contains a collection of memoirs and writings from a group of people who were involved in or affected by the Vietnam War, in some fashion. Many of the people are my personal friends and/or people I have become acquainted with through my writing. There are thousands of other stories out there, and each one deserves to be heard.

This collection of stories includes authors, reporters, military veterans and civilians alike. Each story reflects an effect or experience of the Vietnam War by that particular individual, and yet at the same time is common to many of us who were affected by or involved in the war.

Some people have multiple stories from those days. I, like many other military veterans of the war, also have memories as a civilian during our long military involvement in Vietnam. Many of my military experiences appear in some of my earlier blog stories.

I believe everyone from that era has a story to tell, and I am honored to pass on these memoirs and writings which have been shared with me.

I believe you will enjoy them.

Part 1: War and Military Stories

JOE GALLOWAY

Joseph Galloway is an award-winning author, newspaper correspondent and columnist. His service during the Vietnam War earned him a bronze star for heroic actions during the battle of the Ia Drang Valley. Along with General Hal Moore, Joe co-authored "We Were Soldiers Once and Young," along with the sequel "We are Soldiers, Still; A Journey Back to the Battlefields of Vietnam." I am proud to count Joe among my friends. He kindly provided this quote to set the tone for our article:

"We who have seen war will never stop seeing it, in the silence of the night we will always hear the screams…so this is our story…For we were soldiers once and young."

Joseph Galloway, Vietnam War Correspondent and Author

Part 1: War and Military Stories

JoAnn Forrester

JoAnn Forrester is an author and business consultant. She has shared her thoughts on those days, and the aftermath.

Vietnam!

Vietnam, the war of the Baby Boomer generation, left a multitude of raw scars on our national conscience. A war, where 9.2 million American men and women served throughout the world, mostly during an eleven year period (Jan. 1, 1965 – March 28, 1973), as warriors and peace keepers.

Of that number, 2,709, 918 Americans, or about 3.5 percent of the boomer generation served in Vietnam, leaving 58,228 killed, 304,705 wounded and 2,400 listed as missing at the end of the war.

For those who came home from the war…it really never ended. There were no parades, no thank you, no you did a great job…for most there was rejection, blame and hostility. Coming home and adjusting to an uncivil world took its toll on our men, women and their families. Many problems resulting from PTSD and Agent Orange were ignored and/or denied by the Veteran Administration and US government thus creating more hardships that resulted in early deaths, suicide, disabilities and alienation.

Slowly we have begun to deal with our past and try to soothe the wounds. Each man and woman who served has a story to be told and heard.

A salute to all that served.

JoAnn R. Forrester

Part 1: War and Military Stories

MAJOR MICHAEL O'DONNELL

Major Michael O'Donnell was a helicopter pilot killed in action near Dak To, Vietnam in March of 1970. Although I did not know Major O'Donnell we were in Vietnam at the same time, and in some of the same places. This is a poem he penned several months before his death.

If you are able,

save them a place

inside of you

and save one backward glance

when you are leaving

for the places they can

no longer go.

Be not ashamed to say

you loved them,

though you may

or may not have always.

Take what they have left

and what they have taught you

with their dying

and keep it with your own.

And in that time

when men decide and feel safe

to call the war insane,

take one moment to embrace

those gentle heroes

you left behind.

Major Michael Davis O'Donnell, 1 January 1970, RIP

ART REAGAN

Art Reagan and I became acquainted through my writing. Art pens many short articles himself. He is an avid historian and a very thorough researcher. One of his earlier works also appears on my blog. Art has shared some of his thoughts for our article:

"Vietnam is more than a country, more than a war. It's the stuff 60s' kids are made of and will be till the day we die. More than anything else, it changed our culture and the way we think about ourselves. Let's face it, there was a draft on and many young people—confronted with mandatory military service in a country no one had ever heard of—were unwilling to trade the comfort of familiar surroundings to defend a South East Asian country from the specter of a communist takeover. Since then, of course, we've all become experts at defending our views of the war and the recollections we are allowed to share."

Art Reagan, Vietnam Era Veteran, Veteran of the unseen war in Vietnam and Southeast Asia.

Part 1: War and Military Stories

JOYCE FAULKNER

Joyce Faulkner is the co-owner of The Red Engine Press. She is also an award winning author and long-time board member of The Military Writer's Society of America. (MWSA) In addition to being my publisher, I am proud to have Joyce as a friend. Joyce shared this writing with us:

I was born to hate war. There, I've said it. You see, my father was a combat Marine who fought all thirty-six days of the Battle of Iwo Jima. His squad was killed off to a man, except for him. Twice. That experience colored the rest of his life—and most of mine. He had nightmares. He screamed in the night if my mother rolled over and accidentally touched him. He sobbed with pride and sorrow every time he saw the film of those guys raising the flag on top of Suribachi. He made me crouch down under the picture window lest the "Japs" shoot me through it. He beat my mother—and me.

When I was ten, he planned to kill us and his parents. Fortunately, my grandfather and uncle wrestled the gun away from him and the cops put him in a straight jacket. He spent at least a year in the hospital writing letters filled with ghosts and anger and paranoia—and sent them to my mother. Inexplicable, unintelligible letters that she hid unopened in her jewelry box where I found them after her death years later.

In the 1960s, I was a college student. Period. I didn't protest the war in Vietnam, although an unending stream of friends, classmates and acquaintances did. That was because an unending stream of our friends, classmates, and acquaintances were going to Vietnam and an unequal number of them were coming home safe and sound. Throughout all of this, my philosophical explorations never veered left or right of center. Neither abyss offered much comfort.

My interactions with young men making the transition from warrior back to student were sorrowful, tender and empathetic. I hung out with them. Held their hands. Listened to their stories. Grieved with them. Wrote about them. Welcomed them home.

However, I had one rule. One absolutely unbreakable rule. I didn't actually date service men—or veterans of war. Any war.

I had a horror of falling in love with a man like my father, who I adored, feared, and worried about day and night. Most especially, I didn't want to wake up in the middle of the night to find my husband pacing the house with a loaded rifle. I didn't want to find him in the bathroom crying until he threw up. I didn't want to sit outside a hospital room while he had shock treatments. I didn't want any more of that. No way.

But then I found the perfect man. We studied together in the library. We both wanted to travel. We both were straight arrow kids. No guns. No smoking. No drugs. Okay, so he drank beer. Our dates consisted of dinner out, a trip to a hobby store to buy a model airplane kit, back to his apartment to watch Star Trek—and then the rest of the evening assembling and painting the model. The best thing about him was that he hadn't passed the physical. You know. THE physical. So, eventually, with all of these special qualities, I let myself fall in love with him.

We had been married three years and six months and were living in Japan when the letter arrived. He'd been drafted. He was one week from turning twenty-six. The bastards at the draft board decided "latent sugar diabetes" didn't really exist so they reclassified him and drafted him on the same day. And we had to go home.

I was terrified. I cried. I prayed. I begged. I threw up. But no, he wanted to go home and report. He really *was* a straight arrow, you see. It was Thursday. He had to report on Monday. He packed what he could while I sulked. We telegraphed the draft board that we were out of the country but that we were coming. Despite all the complications, we arrived back in the States late Sunday. In the middle of the night, we got a phone call from Japan. The draft board, on hearing we were hurrying home, had given him a break. He had ninety days to join something. We spent the reprieve arranging for our things to be shipped home—and joining the Air Force.

I was still mad the day we showed up for him to enlist and immediately be sent to off to Basic Training. My fear—that I'd have to stay with my parents and endure my dad's heartbreaking craziness again—was assuaged when my husband arranged for me to stay with his perfectly lovely and sane parents.

He was the oldest inductee that day so he had to carry the orders. By the time we arrived at the airport, my heart was pounding.

"Don't let this change you," I begged.

"I won't," he promised.

We were hugging when the plane taxied up to the gate. He tucked the envelope with the papers under one arm and turned to face the passengers as they came through a sliding glass door. The last passenger through was a business man in an expensive suit. Without a word or even a moan, he dropped his briefcase and fell against me…knocking me backwards. His head crunched when it hit the marble floor. Lying face down at my feet, he released his urine and died.

I screamed. My husband dropped the manila envelope filled with all the draftees' papers, rolled the man over and loosened his tie. "Sir? Sir?"

The airline called for the inductees to board first. The young draftees gathered around the prostrate man, eyes wide.

"Sir?"

"Johnny, he's dead," I said to my husband.

The airline called them again.

Johnny stood up. His face had already changed. He picked up the envelope and squared his shoulders. Then he turned—and with the younger draftees following behind him like puppies—went through the gate.

I sat down beside the dead man, realizing that I'd already changed too.

The loud speaker blared. A crowd formed around me. Some blurry someone tried to say something to me. His lips moved but I couldn't understand him. I was still staring at the dead man on the floor, when paramedics hurried up and checked his vitals. "I'm sorry about your father," one of them touched my arm. "He's passed."

That got through to me and I cried—great, open-mouthed sobs—as the plane took off with my husband.

"That's not my father." I pointed at the corpse and blubbered. "I don't know that man. *My* daddy's a Marine."

Joyce K Faulkner, Author of **In the Shadow of Suribachi**, **Windshift**, **Vala's Bed**, **USERNAME**, **Garrison Avenue** *and other books available on Amazon*

Part 1: War and Military Stories

PHILIP CAPUTO

Philip Caputo is a Vietnam War Veteran and an award-winning author. His book "A Rumor of War" is considered to be one of the finest writings on the Vietnam War. I am proud that Phil has shared this excerpt with us.

"Everything rotted and corroded there: bodies, boot leather, canvas, metal, morals. Scorched by the sun, wracked by the wind and rain of the monsoon, fighting in alien swamps and jungles, our humanity rubbed off of us just as the protective bluing rubbed off the barrels of our rifles."

Philip Caputo, **A Rumor of War**

Ric Hunter is a Vietnam War Veteran, a retired USAF pilot, and a Red Engine Press award-winning author. His stirring book "FIREHAMMER" has been widely acclaimed.

The Phabulous Phantom in Vietnam

In May of 1975, I was privileged to fly the F-4D "Phantom" as a pilot in the last battle of the Vietnam War. In that battle, I avenged the loss of my high school best friend, a Marine, killed by an NVA sniper near the Demilitarized Zone in '66.

What's it like to fly the world's leading fighter aircraft against an enemy? This enemy was trying to kill some 150 Marines trapped on an island in the Gulf of Thailand. Flying the aircraft at this point is instinctive, I can't remember any particular inputs as I rolled it over on my back and dove at the ground at 500 MPH. What I do remember is making sure I had the weapon switches and gun sight set and above all—not wanting to blow any marines to kingdom come. They were at times in hand-to-hand combat in the jungle. That meant we had to get very close to the bad-guys, Cambodian Khmer Rouge of the "Killing Fields" fame. My wingman and I put 78 rockets and 20 MM cannon on the enemy and ultimately helped free those trapped Marines.

The F-4 was a beast, and in the right hands was lethal. Over 5000 of them were produced by McDonnell-Douglas and the Phabulous Phantom was considered the "work horse" of the Vietnam War.

Ric Hunter is a retired Air Force fighter pilot who wrote a historical fiction novel about this period in the war. It is entitled **FIREHAMMER**, *and was nominated for a Pulitzer Prize. It is available on Amazon.*

Part 1: War and Military Stories

JIMMY FOX

Jimmy Fox, a U.S. Army Vietnam War Veteran and I became acquainted at a Veteran's event some years ago, and I am proud to count him among my friends. Jimmy has penned several writings on the war, No Peace is an excellent one.

NO PEACE

We came home nearly forty years ago to a place that we didn't know, and that didn't know us. We tried our best to fit in, to go back in time, trying to return to who we were and what we had been just a few short years earlier. For most of us, it didn't work. The world that we knew, and that thought they knew us, was no longer there, gone, along with our innocence, and a lot of our friends. Many things, and in some cases, people, that just a few years earlier had meant so much to us, meant nothing now—and the feeling was mutual. Often, the one who had promised to wait forever, didn't... but we never knew 'til we came home. Sometimes, even churches that we went to before didn't want us sitting in the same pews with "good" people on Sunday. After all... WE had blood on our hands...Things like this are hard to forget, or forgive.

Our "before 'Nam" buddies, the ones who didn't go, weren't anymore. The ones that would still talk to us just wanted to know what we had "DONE" over there. And then didn't want to listen when we told them. They soon figured out that we weren't puttin' up with their bullshit, and stopped coming around. We had lost friends before... We tried to forget.........

So, time goes by, many of us found someone who accepted us, and was willing to put up with our little "quirks." Soon we had kids, a place to live, and in some instances, after many failed attempts, a pretty decent job. And, we had a dog. (him we could trust) It seemed as if we had everything we needed…………..We almost forgot………..BUT…….

But there was NO PEACE. There was NEVER any PEACE. Not really. Things were just never the same for us. Everyone always wondered why, but they didn't really want to know. Some people said "If it's that Vietnam thing, get over it. It wasn't really a war, and besides it was a long time ago. Grow up." Most people don't deserve to know, most never will. We do.

The people we choose to let into our lives are either like us, or accept us for who we are. We seem to surround ourselves with others, who like us, also cannot forget, yet who we know we can forever, and always, really trust. Those that know what we are about, what is in our hearts, and that share the love we have for each other. WE WILL NEVER FORGET, that's what makes us,………The Vietnam Veteran,……..

BROTHERS FOREVER

Jim Fox. 1st Cav Vietnam War Veteran '67-'68

Emily Strange

Emily Strange, a Vietnam War Donut Dollie, was a writer as well. She passed away in 2016. One of her close friends, fellow Donut Dollie Rene Johnson, was kind enough to provide one of Emily's writings for us.

Donut Dollie

I flew to desolate fire bases
filled with the tools of war
and the men who used them.

It was my mission to raise the morale
of children who had grown old too soon
watching friends die.

It was my calling
to take away fear and replace it with hope;
to return sanity to a world gone insane.

I was the mistress of illusion
as I pulled smiles from the dust and heat,
the magical genie of "back-in-the-world"
as I created laughter in the mud.
But when the show was over
I crawled back into my bottle
and pulled the cork in tightly behind me.

Emily Strange, U.S. Red Cross Donut Dollie,
Vietnam War, RIP

WOMEN OF WAR;
WOMEN OF COURAGE...

She's proof that you can walk through hell, and still be an angel.

R.H.Sin

This article touches on the role that female warriors have played throughout history, culminating with the United States War in Vietnam, and a brief discussion on women in today's military. The article covers some of the more noted women of battle over the centuries and goes over some specific accounts of female fighters during the Vietnam.

Not Uncommon

Historically, men bore the brunt of battle during periods of war. However, many women also stepped up (or down, whatever the case may have been) to fight for God, family and the homeland. Female fighters were much more common than I was aware of, so rather than attempting to cover the formidable number of women warriors over the eons, I have highlighted several fighting women of distinction here.

Many barbarian tribes before, during and after the Roman era employed female fighters not only on an as needed basis, but also as modus operandi — a standard method of operation if you will. Viking women, for example, routinely wielded the sword, and took part in the raucous victory rituals as well. Women in Native American tribes fought on an as needed basis throughout their history.

The Trojan Wars

The Trojan Wars, steeped in Greek mythology, supposedly took place between 1260 – 1180 BC. The wars, as written, were waged between Greeks and Spartans including one fought over Helen, who had been spirited off by the Greeks. As legend goes, both the Greeks and Spartans employed female archers known as Amazons. These Amazons were originally from the Steppes of Central Asia and were extremely war like and ferocious. Although the Amazons wielded all weapons at their disposal, they were known for their exceptional prowess in archery. Whosoever employed these archers most effectively often won the battle at hand.

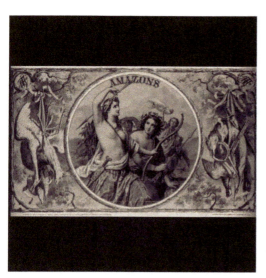

Part 1: War and Military Stories

THE TRUNG SISTERS OF VIETNAM

The Trung Sisters, 40 – 43 AD, are credited with driving the invading Chinese out of Vietnam. Emperor Wu of the Chinese Han Dynasty annexed part of Vietnam in 111 BC.

The Trung sisters grew up in a rural area to a family steeped in martial arts. No wall flowers, when they came of age they studied the art of war—and organized a rebellion against the Northern invaders. Although initially successful, they and their followers were defeated by a huge Chinese army in 43 AD. As a result, sisters are said to have committed suicide by drowning themselves. Despite their defeat and deaths, they became an inspirational legacy which ultimately culminated in the permanent expulsion of the Chinese.

BOUDICA

The once mighty Roman Empire ruled over Britain for almost five hundred years. In fact, Roman roads, fortresses and ruins are in evidence in Great Britain to this day. However, the Roman reign would not always be an easy one thanks in no small part to Boudica, The Warrior Queen. Records are unclear as to the year of Boudica's actual birth. However, she died in 61 AD. Boudica was born into a royal family of the Iceni people of Britannia, though under Roman Rule. She was reported to have exhibited great intelligence at an early age—and despite her gender, she became an impressive leader of men.

Because of heavy taxation and abuse of the local citizenry, the Romans were increasingly unpopular in Britain. While they waged war on the Druids in another part of Britannia, Boudica united her Iceni with another large Tribe. With an estimated two hundred and thirty thousand warriors, Boudica attacked the occupying Roman force. She and her allies overwhelmed and slaughtered between sixty and seventy thousand Romans in a remarkably short period of time. The victory was short lived however, as the Roman leader Suetonius quickly regrouped Roman forces and, despite being heavily outnumbered, he crushed the rebellious Britains, who were then themselves slaughtered like ants. Boudica was either killed in battle or took her own life—neither of which has ever been confirmed. However her exploits live on in legend and folklore.

THE AMERICAN WAR IN VIETNAM 1963 – 1975 *1

Female Fighters of Note during the Vietnam War

Over the course of the Vietnam War there were many Vietnamese women on both sides of the hostilities that fought bravely for their family, and their homeland. Here are just a few of them.

Ho Thi Que

Had I known of Ho Thi Que, my dim outlook regarding the outcome of the war might have been different. Que, known as "The Tiger Lady" fought with the Black Tiger battalion of the South Vietnamese Army. Although she was assigned duty as a medic, her ferociousness in battle was legendary. Moreover, she would attack any South Vietnamese soldiers she found looting or abusing South Vietnamese civilians—an unfortunate practice by some in the Army of South Vietnam. Ho Thi Que wore a pair of .45 caliber pistols on each hip and a helmet painted with the head of a tiger. Tragically, Que was shot and killed by her husband after she attacked him with a knife over his affair with another woman.

Nguyen Thi Hien

A North Vietnamese female fighter of note was Nguyen Thi Hien. Hien, at the age of 19, became the leader of a military squad in Yen Vuc, Ham Rong district (aka Dragon Jaw bridge), in Thanh Hoa province. Hien's comrades had to dig her out four times after her bunker was collapsed under explosive waves of U.S. B-52 bombs, and each time Hien lived on to rally anti-aircraft forces attempting to shoot down the huge aircraft.

Hien survived the war and still resides in Northern Vietnam.

Apache

A Viet Cong cadre known as "Apache" became infamous during the Vietnam War. Apache, a platoon commander, sniper and interrogator, was notorious for torturing her victims who she either seduced or captured at gunpoint. She would torment her captives for hours, hideously mutilating them before they finally succumbed to death. Eventually, Apache was killed by U.S. Marine sniper, Carlos Hathcock; also known as "White Feather." Hathcock, a legend in his own right, later reported that killing Apache was the most gratifying mission he had undertaken during his time in Vietnam.

The Author's Experience with a Female Fighter of the Vietnam War

On a personal note, one of the more memorable incidents from my time in Vietnam involved the fate of a young Vietcong woman who had been mortally wounded during a B-52 bombing raid near our base at Phu Cat. American soldiers found the woman, actually a girl of no more than fourteen or fifteen, as she lay dying amongst the rubble. They relayed her story to us when they arrived back at our base at Phu Cat, recalling how as a medic tried to comfort the girl she had put her arms around the man and asked him to hug her. As the medic complied with her wish the brave young girl spoke her last words; "I want to be held by a man before I die."

A sobering event for all who witnessed or heard of the incident, it profoundly affected my feelings on the likely outcome of the war. For all the Vietnamese whom I had encountered during my time at the Phu Cat airbase, as well as those we interacted with out on the road; none had demonstrated any such passion regarding the war. As a matter of fact, many of the Vietnamese I came to know seemed fairly ambivalent about the progress of the war, and even somewhat dubious regarding which side they favored. And though many of them seemingly appreciated what America was trying to do on their behalf, I had the marked feeling that a significant number of them would also be happy if we were to leave the very next day.

My lifelong friend Jim Booth, a serious boxing aficionado, often said "Always bet on the hungry fighter. You'll win most of your bets that way." In my opinion, for whatever reason, the Viet Cong and the North Vietnamese Army (NVA) were "hungrier" than the Army of South Vietnam, the South Vietnamese government and those that supported them.

The U.S. Military Today

Since the first Gulf War back in the 1990s and moving along to the current War in Afghanistan and Iraq; women in today's military are taking on combat roles which were traditionally handled by men. The women who filled these positions have done an outstanding job—many sacrificing life and limb for their fellow soldiers and for their country. God bless them, and God bless America.

* 1. The time period of heaviest U.S. military involvement in Vietnam

SOLDIERS OF GOD ...

"Some people regard the meek man as one who will not put up a fight for anything but will let others run over him... In fact from human experience we know that to accomplish anything good a person must make an effort; and making an effort is putting up a fight against the obstacles."

Father Emil Kapaun, U.S. Army, KIA Korean War, Congressional Medal of Honor Recipient

As Christmas comes around, old memories stir regarding some of the activities I took part in while serving with the U.S. Air Force in Vietnam.

In addition to ministering to the spiritual needs of all GIs in the area, our military chaplains at the Phu Cat Air Base in Binh Dinh Province also ministered to the spiritual as well as the material needs of Vietnamese in the area. I took part in two of the programs spearheaded by these chaplains. One involved helping out with the local orphanages, (see my earlier blog story The Orphans, February 2016) the other involved helping out at the leprosarium in Qui Nhon. Although some of us volunteers were only involved at Christmas time, the chaplains tended to the orphanages and leprosarium year round.

At the leprosarium, the chaplains would bring any number of needed goods, including medical supplies, food and spiritual items. They would go through each small hut and minister to the poor souls who were struck by the horrific malady of leprosy. On the one trip that I assisted the chaplains in this effort, I helped load and unload trucks. I'm ashamed to say that along with several others who came to help, I did not have the courage to go into any of the huts along with the chaplains, fearing the dreaded contagion. We waited outside near our vehicles, catching a glimpse of some of those poor souls as they walked in and out of their huts.

Photo courtesy of Byron Mccalman

In addition to administering to the spiritual needs of GIs and helping the locals with their different programs, the chaplains also took the job of mental health counselor and therapist. Lonely, tired and scared GIs often sought out the chaplains who would give freely of their time and services.

The base chaplains would also go out into the field to assist other overwhelmed chaplains in ministering to the needs of troops whose dangerous lives often brought them face to face with the end. Along with holding field services, the chaplains counseled war weary grunts and provided last rites as needed.

The chaplains also fulfilled the difficult role of providing a moral compass during the Vietnam War, often speaking out against activities which they deemed immoral or contrary to God's word. For many years they railed against the habit of collecting enemy ears for trophies or body counts, successfully curbing that practice in many areas.

Part 1: War and Military Stories

Photo courtesy of Bernie Weisz

On many occasions, the chaplains found themselves fighting right alongside the GIs they ministered to, defending themselves and members of their flock. During the course of the Vietnam War, fifteen U.S. military chaplains were killed in the line of duty—and many more were wounded. Many chaplains earned various medals for bravery and honor including three who were awarded the Congressional Medal of Honor.

Congressional Medal of Honor recipient Father Charles Watters, U.S. Army, served two tours in Vietnam. He was awarded the Air Medal and Bronze Star during his first tour in 1964. During his second tour in 1967, while retrieving wounded men and administering last rites, Father Watters was killed.

Congressional Medal of Honor recipient Father Vincent Capodanno, U.S Navy, served with the U.S. Marines in Vietnam. He also exposed himself repeatedly while retrieving Marines wounded or killed in action. Capodanno himself was killed while administering last rites to a wounded Marine.

Congressional Medal of Honor recipient Father Charles Liteky, U.S. Army, served in Vietnam in 1967. He was severely wounded while carrying many wounded men to safety. After the war, Liteky left the priesthood. He joined the anti-war movement and left his Congressional Medal of Honor at the Vietnam War Memorial (The Wall) in Washington D.C. in 1986.

The clergy who served in the U.S. military in the Vietnam War provided a tremendous service for all who were there.

"I am young, I am twenty years old; yet I know nothing of life but despair, death, fear, and fatuous superficiality cast over an abyss of sorrow. I see how peoples are set against one another, and in silence, unknowingly, foolishly, obediently, innocently slay one another."

Erich Maria Remarque, **All Quiet on the Western Front**.

A Well for Phu Cat

Humor comes at us in many places, and it is most often welcome.

Joe

I was a member of the United States Air Force from 1968 to 1972. I served at Phu Cat Airbase, Republic of Vietnam, from January of 1970 to January of 1971.

Because I kept requesting a transfer out of supply into civil engineering, when I first arrived at Phu Cat I was assigned to a civil engineering detail headed by the Red Horse Squadron. The detail involved building a water pumping station by the river near Phu Cat so the villagers would not have to hand carry water from the river in buckets, as they had been doing. A dangerous endeavor, particularly after the sun went down. Unfortunately, because of Vietcong intervention that project ended in disaster and was subsequently canceled. The Civil Engineering squadron soon redeployed to Bien Hoa and as I had no acquired skills as of yet, I was transferred back to supply and remained at Phu Cat.

Within weeks of the incident, the Phu Cat village chief started pestering the base commander again. The village needed running water. In time, a solution was developed—a well would be drilled by the main gate at the Phu Cat airbase which was on the northern edge of the village. Since the main gate was heavily guarded twenty four hours a day, the risk from Vietcong sabotage would be greatly reduced.

Soon U.S. Air Force maintenance teams were hard at work. They drilled the well, built an open-air shelter around it, tested it and released it for use. A formal dedication ceremony with base and village leaders was planned.

However the first morning after completion, before the dedication ceremony was to take place, an older village woman walked purposely out to the new well, with several younger women and children in tow. U.S.A.F. personnel on hand watched with curiosity, expecting her to be the first customer to collect a nice fresh bucket of water.

To their astonishment, the old woman entered the shelter, scooted her black pants down, hopped on the well and defecated. About half the men on hand started yelling, while the other half roared with laughter while cheering the old woman on. A call was placed to the engineering squadron, who immediately arranged a meeting with village elders. The elders were ordered to instruct all villagers what the well was intended for, and how to properly use it. A sign was put up with a picture of a person defecating in the well with a large black slash through it, intending to convey what NOT to do in the well.

After getting bleached out, the well was released to the village and soon villagers began using it for its intended purpose, although according to rumor the old mama-san would sneak in at night and use it as her private toilet. As for myself…I made it a point never to drink from it!

NOTE: This story was published in MWSA Dispatches, Winter 2016

My First Week in Vietnam

The meat has been brought to the tiger.

Vietnamese saying

A Serious Change of Scenery

I served in the United States Air Force from 1968 to 1972. I served in Vietnam from January of 1970 to January of 1971. I was assigned to base supply, however from early on I aspired to transfer to a unit where I could learn a more marketable skill with perhaps more interesting work.

Before serving in Vietnam, I was stationed at Grand Forks Air Force Base in North Dakota. While at Grand Forks I had the opportunity to transfer into the nuclear weapons field. After several months of background checks and aptitude testing, I was approved for the program. However due to circumstances beyond my control, conditions suddenly changed and my status in the program was put on hold.

The year being 1969 with the war in Southeast Asia raging, I soon received orders for duty in Vietnam. As soon as I got to my duty station at Phu Cat Airbase in the Central Highlands of Vietnam I was told to report to the Red Horse Squadron on base. The Red Horse Squadron is the U.S. Air Force equivalent of the U.S. Navy Seabees. They perform any number of tasks required to get a unit up and running, all over the globe. I was surprised, but happy because I felt I would be transferred into the unit and would learn a good trade, with interesting work.

Hot, Laborious Work

The village was dirt poor.

Reporting for duty my first day of work, I learned that our unit would be building a water pumping station for the village of Phu Cat. The village had minimal electrical service, but no running water. Village women and children were responsible for toting buckets of water from the river to the village as needed. This was, at times, very dangerous because the area was frequented by leopards, tigers and many poisonous snakes, not to mention Vietcong. (VC) This was one of the base commander's "do gooder" projects and as such was given a high priority.

Tigers and leopards posed a real threat to the villagers.

Another FNG (new arrival) and I were tasked with carrying bags of cement from the truck to the bottom of the steep river bank where the pumping station was to be built. It typically took new arrivals in Vietnam about a month to get acclimated to the hot, steamy environment, not to mention the mosquitoes, leeches, ticks…and VC.

Eager beavers, we launched ourselves into our work, moving twenty or thirty bags of cement down the hill in the first few hours. However, as the day grew warmer and our unconditioned bodies weakened, the task soon took it's toll on us. We took to rolling the ninety-pound bags of dry cement down the hill, however some broke open, raising the ire of the grizzled old Master Sergeant who was running the job.

It wasn't much of a river

And sure enough, around eleven o: clock, my partner first, then I, were both overcome by heat and exertion. He collapsed and rolled down the hill, tumbling like an out of control freight car. My legs gave out beneath me as well, causing me to slide down the embankment feet first. A few of the men in the outfit stopped their work momentarily and set us half in the river and half out so we could cool off and rest. We laid like that for about a half hour, nauseous and groggy. After we recovered, slowly but surely, we resumed our work and managed to get the remaining bags of cement down the hill and ready for mixing. It was a brutal exhausting day for the two of us, but we got through it.

The work detail returned to the base after about fourteen hours, intending to resume work early the next morning. The Master Sergeant praised our efforts and handed out cold Black Label beers to all. Relaxing and joking around, my partner and I felt proud, as we were now made to feel part of the group, sharing C rations and cold crisp beer with our new mates. We slept like rocks that night and again reported for duty at five thirty the next morning, sore as hell but ready to go.

A VC Calling Card

Rolls of concertina wire gave us a measure of protection the villagers did not have.

Arriving at the work site just a mile or so outside the base, we were in for a surprise. All of the new construction that we had started the previous day was demolished, the newly-poured cement footings smashed, the wooden posts and beams torn down and scattered. The few hand tools that we had left were also either broken or taken from the site.

We just stood there for a time, a bit stunned. Collectively, we realized the local VC had paid us a visit. Our effort, not surprisingly, was not welcome by them. Anything that made the U.S. look good, also made the rebels look bad. They weren't going to stand still for it. Now furious, the old Master Sergeant stood glowering. "You men salvage what you can, take an inventory of what we need and start pouring new footings. I'll go report to the Major."

As ordered, we took stock of the situation, noting what additional material we would need. We then started pouring new cement footings right over the old damaged ones. The Sarge returned, this time with the Major who wanted to see the damage for himself. With them, they brought several thermos bottles of coffee, cans of soda, candy bars and a truck full of new supplies. The sarge let go with a few expletives, "We're gonna rebuild it and the hell with them!" Everyone pitched in that day, even the Major. We were furious at the VC and it was reflected in the spirit in which we worked. Villagers came down and helped as well, bringing bottles of rice wine and "33" beer for everyone.

My partner and I were able to get through the day, without any fatigue related issues like we had experienced the first day, taking breaks with the rest of the group only as needed. The whole unit was fired up and worked all day repairing what had been damaged, and then some. When we left the site late in the evening, the Phu Cat village chief agreed to post a guard to prevent a re-occurrence of what had happened the night before. We felt good about our effort and celebrated with cold beers once again. We had a nice steak fry as well, compliments of the Officer's and NCO club.

A Grim Scene Awaits Us

For the Vietnamese, terror was a constant companion

The next morning we left the base with a bit of trepidation, and our arrival at the work site confirmed our worst fears. The VC had again paid us a visit during the night. The guard the village chief had promised was nowhere to be found, and what we did find unsettled us considerably. Instead of just destroying the new work we had accomplished the VC sent us a much stronger signal. As we moved down the embankment, a loud drone filled our ears. We gasped, and stood stunned by what greeted us at the work site. Instead of destroying and stealing our materials as they had previously done, the small enclosure we had completed was now packed with the bodies of villagers the VC had killed. In the hot steamy environment, immense clouds of flies roiled over the bodies, which had already started to decompose.

It was a horrid scene and many of us wretched at the site. After the initial shock, we mostly stood quiet, with even the grizzled old Master Sergeant standing mute. Upon regaining his composure, the Master Sergeant directed one man to alert the village chief. We left two armed men at the scene and returned to the base. After hearing the report from the Master Sergeant, the Major contacted the base commander who pulled the plug on the operation. He felt the effort was not worth the deaths of anymore villagers.

And Back to Supply Again

The ROK bunker where I spent most of my last two months in Vietnam.

A week later the Red Horse squadron at Phu Cat was redeployed to Bien Hoa, a base in another part of Vietnam. My partner and I, having acquired no skills were transferred back to our original units and remained at Phu Cat. I spent the rest of my tour assigned to base supply, spending much of my time working in the warehouse on base, moving materials via truck to other military facilities in the area, and humping cargo on aircraft all around the Central Highlands of South Vietnam. I spent the last two months in the ROK (Republic of Korea) bunker just outside the western perimeter of the base.

Success at Last!

The main gate at Phu Cat became the home of the village well.

A few months after our attempt to build the water pump failed, a well was drilled near the main gate of the Phu Cat airbase. (Reference my earlier story, "A Well for Phu Cat") The well was within easy walking distance of the village and being near the main gate was protected twenty-four hours a day. Thus, the water problem for the village of Phu Cat was finally solved.

Part 1: War and Military Stories

THE ROKs
REPUBLIC OF KOREA
SOLDIERS IN VIETNAM

President Johnson did not want the war to broaden. He wanted the North Vietnamese to leave their brothers in the south alone.

William Westmoreland

RECRUITED ALLIES

ROKs preparing for action.

Many American GIs who served in Vietnam had contact of one kind or another with troops from South Korea, commonly referred to as the "ROKs." The Republic of Korea, a staunch ally of the U.S., sent some 335,000 troops to fight in South Vietnam from 1965 to 1973. Of those 335,000 troops, some 5,500 were killed in action while over 11,000 were wounded. Though the South Korean Army contributed most of those troops, members of South Korea's Marines, Air Force and Navy also participated in the war.

Part 1: War and Military Stories

Johnson desperately needed support for the war.

As one of the participants of Lyndon B. Johnson's "Many Flags" campaign, South Korea became the largest foreign presence in Vietnam, after the United States.

Controversies Arise

The South Korean government was not anxious to send troops to Vietnam but did so for economic reasons, and more importantly, because it feared the United States would transfer many of its own troops from South Korea to Vietnam, if they did not comply with Johnson's request. Even so, South Korea was granted specific sums of money for each South Korean troop deployed to South Vietnam, along with regularly scheduled "general" payments to the South Korean government for the duration of the war. As part of the agreement, the U.S. also agreed to purchase many war materials from South Korea and contracted with South Koreans for many other war related services during the course of the war. These activities prompted many U.S. politicians and citizens to decry the actions as nothing more than the hiring of mercenaries to fight Johnson's war, as well as shelling out poorly veiled bribes for foreign support.

Other problems arose with the South Vietnamese military who largely detested the Koreans, believing them to be interlopers and bullies.

South Korean Soldiers and Marines, known for their toughness were accused of various atrocities throughout the war, and to this day, the government of Vietnam is still attempting to press charges against the South Koreans for actions that occurred during their time there.

Part 1: War and Military Stories

The ROKs held no sympathy for the enemy.

Admiration and Respect, from the U.S. Military

The ROKs aided the U.S. military in every way.

Despite the controversies surrounding their participation in the war, the U.S. military held the South Koreans in high regard and U.S. GIs who served with the ROKs (me included) hold many favorable memories of them.

The two ROK army divisions that served in Vietnam were the "White Horse Division" and the "Capitol Division," more commonly known as the "Tiger Division."

Part 1: War and Military Stories

Tiger Division Patch

My involvement with the Koreans was with the "Tiger Division" which had two camps just outside the Phu Cat Airbase perimeter.

The Phu Cat perimeter was frequently probed by VC and the NVA.

At Phu Cat, the "Tigers" conducted both passive operations, including defensive positions along our perimeter, as well as aggressive operations including search and destroy patrols in the general area surrounding the Phu Cat Airbase.

As more and more elements of the 173rd Airborne were pulled back during President Nixon's Vietnamization program, the Phu Cat Airbase assumed more and more responsibility for its own protection. Security police and augmantees (volunteers) patrolled the base perimeter 24 hours a day. The local Vietcong often probed the perimeter, sending sappers in to inflict damage whenever they could. While Air Force base defenses performed the passive defense, they were not trained or equipped to go out on patrols, seeking out Vietcong and North Vietnamese soldiers. The ROKs, on the other hand, performed that task very well.

The ROKs and Me

The main ROK compound outside Phu Cat Airbase southern perimeter.

I first became associated with the ROKs when I spent time in their main camp outside of our south perimeter learning the martial art of Tae Kwon Do. Larger and stronger than the Vietnamese, the ROKs were tough, disciplined and extremely dedicated in the application of their practice of karate. Watching them as they trained and sparred we became quite impressed with their physical prowess. Few Americans could match their abilities in hand to hand fighting.

I eventually earned a yellow belt in Tai Kwon Do, but never took it any farther; I was not what you would call a "natural" in that endeavor. Some of my peers became quite enthralled with the martial art, earning various degrees of black belts. They would spend their off duty hours with the Koreans, training and sparring. Our non-com at the time would often chide us over our involvement in the activity. He called us "chimbee artists" after the sound we made when we executed our moves.

When I had about three months left of my tour of duty in Vietnam, I began spending much of my time in the Korean bunker just outside of our Western perimeter. My two best friends whose tours were over had already left Vietnam. With Nixon's Vietnamization program in full swing, my previous duty station required a skeleton crew only, leaving me a ship without a navy, so to speak. Recruited for other duty, I spent about one month loading and unloading cargo on C-130 and C-47 aircraft. I flew all around the Central Highlands of Vietnam during that time. That was great duty for me; I especially enjoyed my one-week stay at Nha Trang, which had a beautiful beach for swimming and surfing.

However when my flying days ended, I still had little to do and was pretty much in charge of my own activities. I took my R&R to Hong Kong (much enjoyed) but when I came back, I still had no workstation to report to on a regular basis so I started hanging with my old friends, the ROKs.

The ROK bunker where I spent most of my last two months in-country.

The ROKs on our Western perimeter maintained a small, less than platoon size bunker, and because of my earlier association with them, I now found myself charged with making sure they had everything they needed that our Airbase could provide. (They finally found something for me to do so I'd leave them alone) I felt this was worthy duty and I also enjoyed it.

Each morning I would walk over to the ROK compound just outside of our Western perimeter, and spend most of the day there. The ROK Lieutenant in charge would greet me on arrival after which we would discuss any number of topics. Protocol was important to the ROKs and it was necessary for me to spend whatever time the Lieutenant required, discussing whatever subject he liked. As a recent convert to Christianity, the Lieutenant liked to discuss religion. Being a Luke-warm disciple of religion, my participation in the discussion was based primarily on manners and military protocol.

Kim Jun-Ki and I

The rest of my day at the Korean compound would be spent in any number of ways at my new duty station. One of the Korean soldiers and I became close friends over time and we were inseparable during my time there. Kim Jun-Ki and I fished and swam in the little river that ran by their compound, and shared family histories as well. He had a sister named Jun-Ja and he hoped to engineer a marriage between us. Another time, another place perhaps, but I wasn't ready for a marriage based on correspondence, so I held him off on that one. Kim and I kept in contact for several years after we both left Vietnam and after all these years I still think of him often, hoping he prospered and did well in life.

For reasons of self-preservation, the local VC usually spared the ROK compound from the mortar and rocket attacks the airbase was subjected to. During my stay with the Koreans, I recall only one or two mortar attacks and the mortars that fell were well short of our little bunker. It was my opinion that the mortars were intended for the airbase and just fell short.

The ROKs went out on patrol about three or four times a week. They would usually patrol the mountains to the west of our base, known as the Phu Cats. The lieutenant often teased me about going out on patrol with them…at least I thought he was teasing until the day he told me it was time for me to go. Not wanting to lose face, I grabbed my gear and went out on the patrol. Fortunately, for me, it was not one of the long-range patrols up in the Phu Cats, but rather just a short two-hour jaunt outside the airbase perimeter. On this particular mission, our patrol encountered no enemy and my short career as a "grunt" left me unharmed. (God bless the grunts!)

A former ROK soldier, now U.S. citizen at one of my book signings.

Before I left Vietnam, my ROK friends held a celebration on my behalf, including fresh fish from the river, Korean OB 10 beer, and, of course, plenty of kimchee. To this day, I fondly remember all of my days and nights with my Korean friends, I still have a fondness for Kimchee have converted some family members and friends and bring some home now and then.

Part 1: War and Military Stories

THE HEART OF A WARRIOR THE SOUL OF A WRITER

Young men, hear an old man to whom old men hearkened when he was young.

Gaius Octavius Thurinus (Augustus)

My friend Jim Northrup recently passed away. Jim and I became acquainted at a veteran's event in which he was a featured speaker. Our mutual background as Vietnam War Veterans who enjoy writing spawned our correspondence and friendship. Like all those fortunate enough to know Jim, I admired him and marveled at his journey through life.

Jim was a proud Ojibwa of the Fond Du Lac band in Northern Minnesota. Shuffled around in his youth by a society trying to make him "white," Jim could have easily succumbed to those negative experiences by choosing a path with a bleak future—but he did not. In spite of the poor hand he was dealt, when he became of age, Jim did something inexplicable to some—he joined the U.S. military. And he chose to become a U.S. Marine, the bravest of the brave. And as a U.S. Marine, Jim was sent to Vietnam.

A vicious war for all, Vietnam was a meat grinder for the U.S. Marines. The brutal terrain, harsh climate and guerrilla type war contributed to horrific casualties for the leathernecks. Fighting an indigenous people attempting to throw off the chains of colonialism, Jim found himself in conflict. In a later story, "Grandmother's Hair," Jim tells of an incident in which a captured Vietcong woman has her head cover removed. Jim could not help notice how the coarse, dark hair resembled that of his grandmother. We can only imagine the inner turmoil Jim was experiencing.

Returning from the cauldron in Southeast Asia, Jim encountered all of the negativity that all returning servicemen from that war experienced. Moreover, Jim went back to the reservation where the similarity between those he had just been fighting, and his own people was very evident. Once again, it could have been easy for Jim to choose a dark path—and for a time he did struggle. But two parts of Jim would eventually pull him out of the abyss—the heart of a warrior and the soul of a writer.

Jim started writing about his experiences in life. And he wrote with humor, compassion, and eloquence. His writing is easy to read. It makes the rest of us mortals feel good. It makes us feel Jim's soul. He wrote stories in the form of books and poetry. And Jim was also an eloquent speaker. His keen wit, humor, and ability to tap into the human soul made him a popular speaker at many events.

Jim was a proud Ojibwa, a proud U.S. Marine, and a proud family man. His Facebook pages were full of his activities with his family, extended family, friends and fellow vets. Whether it was harvesting rice, visiting with fellow veterans, or entertaining his grandchildren, Jim had a look of peace and serenity.

When Jim learned that his time in this life was ending, he handled it with wit, serenity, and humor. He made the rest of us feel good about ourselves.

As for myself, I am happy for having known Jim—and happy that his writings will be around for those in the future to enjoy. And when some kind soul tells me I am a hero, I think of men like Jim and reply, "I do not consider myself a hero, but I have walked among some."

Miigwech, my friend.

Memoirs & Essays of the Vietnam War: 2nd Edition

It is forbidden to kill; therefore all murderers are punished unless they kill in large numbers and to the sound of trumpets.

Voltaire

Introduction

Last month's article featuring a compilation of essays and memoirs of the Vietnam War was hugely popular, having been viewed by well over two thousand readers in less than one month. We also received dozens of kind compliments regarding the article, with many readers suggesting that we post additional writings on the topic, so that is what we have done.

This article, like the first one, is a gathering of essays from a diverse group of people who were affected by the Vietnam War in some way. The group is composed of Veterans and authors as well as some veterans who have become authors.

Two pieces of artwork by Trieu Hoang are also featured. Trieu is a young artist from Vietnam. Trieu and I became acquainted through my writing and I am honored to feature his artwork with this article.

Part 1: War and Military Stories

HAL MOORE

Hal Moore was perhaps the most beloved American officer of the Vietnam War. Hal, along with his friend Joe Galloway, authored "We Were Soldiers Once, and Young" and it's sequel "We are Soldiers Still; A Journey back to the Battlefields of Vietnam." General Moore passed away in 2017.

"There's never been a noble war except in the history books and propaganda movies. It's a bloody, dirty, cruel, costly mistake in almost every case, as it was in this war that would end so badly. But the young soldiers can be and often are noble, selfless, and honorable. They don't fight for a flag or a president or mom and apple pie. When it comes down to it they fight and die for each other, and that is reason enough for them, and for me."

Lieutenant General Harold G. Moore, RIP

Artwork Trieu Hoang

Part 1: War and Military Stories

DR. ERIK VILLARD

Erik Villard & Ken Burns

Erik Villard is a historian at the U.S. Army Center for Military History, specializing in the history of the Vietnam War. Erik is the founder of several Facebook groups which deal with historical events relating to the war. Erik has also been involved in screen projects, such as the PBS series on Vietnam by Ken Burns. As one of my Facebook friends I have enjoyed many of Erik's photos and discussions relating to the war.

Erik has kindly provided this writing:

My interest in military history started at an early age when I started playing with plastic toy soldiers and reading books about WWII and the Civil War. By the time I entered high school, the Vietnam War had become my principal area of study. I was too young to remember the war, but my dad had been in the Air Force during the early 1970s, and I remember living on Travis Air Force Base in California where I could see military aircraft up close. I was drawn to the Vietnam War because it was a complex conflict that defied easy categorization- I also appreciated the vast collection of color images and films that helped bring the conflict to life. Even better, there was a generation of living Vietnam War veterans that I could actually talk to, and as time went on I discovered that

I could use my historical knowledge to help these veterans make more sense of their experiences. Since joining the US Army Center of Military History in 2000, I have committed most of my professional life and a great deal of my personal time to researching the Vietnam War in the hope that my efforts will help those veterans, their families, and the public better understand America's most divisive conflict.

Dr. Erik B. Villard, U.S. Army Center of Military History

Bob Schweitzer

xBob Schweitzer, AKA Bob Smoke

SOLDIER

It hit me in the deepest way…Kris Kristofferson talking about the pro-Vietnam war song he wrote back in the day…when he was in the Army.

He emphasized how his view had dramatically changed.

He stated back then he was "totally seeing the world from the perspective of the soldier."

What is seeing the world from the perspective of the soldier?

Does that go away?

When does it stop?

Could this be my angst?

Can I not let go of my training and my gut?
Will I always have the soldier mind?
A Marine is always a Marine.
I was an Airman.
And a large part of me is still an Airman
Military.

Maybe that is why I cannot publicly protest a war I don't
believe in.
I think of the troops.
I think of when I was in that situation.
How it hurt...
and how I hated them!
How abandoned I felt...
as the rockets blasted,
and the snipers sniped.

We had each other.
Whether we believed in the war or not...
We believed in each other.

~Bob Schweitzer

JOHN PODLASKI

John Podlaski is a Vietnam War Veteran and an award-winning author. John and I became acquainted at a veteran's event several years ago when we were both signing copies of our books. When quizzed on his writing, John offered these comments, which he has kindly shared for our article.

Question: What or who inspired you to start writing? And how long have you been writing?

Actually, my wife can take the credit. Thirty years ago, my mother gifted us with a shoe box containing every letter I had written home while serving in the Vietnam War. We read through the many letters and a personal diary I carried—my wife, intrigued by it all, had a hundred questions. She suggested that I make a short outline based upon the letters and diary and then try to flesh it out so her questions could be answered. I started this project on a manual typewriter and carbon paper, intending to write something no longer than a term paper. However, as more questions and requests for clarification were made, the "term paper" grew. Editing, during this time, required an entire chapter to be retyped in order to maintain proper structure. In early 1980, Atari came out with a game console that offered a word processor, the ability to store data on floppy disks and a dot matrix printer. Purchasing this, I spent the next three months duplicating all the key strokes of the paper into this new computer, then finding it much easier to edit and add to the story.

The manuscript was completed in 1986 and then shopped around to various publishers and entered into contests at various colleges; the story was a finalist at Washington State University's International Literary Awards. I finally located a publisher who was willing to take a chance on my story providing it was rewritten to a third person perspective.

Six months later, the rewrite was half complete and already exceeded the length of the original. I began working a lot of overtime on my job and found that there wasn't any time available to continue my project—this continued for the next year. At that point, I lost interest in the project all together—boxing everything up and moving them to the garage, where they sat for the next twenty years.

In 2009, my wife and I attended our 40th high school reunion—the school was small and we only had sixty students in the graduating class…at least two thirds of them had attended. The last reunion attended was the 20th, and I had forgotten that I had donated two copies of my original manuscript for them to read and pass around. So, I was quite surprised when they asked about the status of that manuscript from long ago. When I told them I stopped the project shortly after that last reunion, they were relentless in their efforts to get me to pick it back up. This persistence continued for the next two or three weeks before I gave in.

The floppy disks could not be converted to Microsoft Word without spending quite a sum of money. My daughter, Nicole, said that if I could print out everything saved, she would get it all into Word. Six weeks later, she handed me a memory stick with both versions.

Nine months later, April 20, 2010, *Cherries* was born as an e-book on Smashwords.com and later as POD on Amazon.com and other platforms.

John Podlaski, award winning author of "Cherries" and "When Can I Stop Running?"

https://cherrieswriter.com

KATHLEEN RODGERS

Fellow writer Kathleen M. Rodgers is a novelist whose stories and essays have appeared in Family Circle Magazine, Military Times, and in anthologies published by McGraw-Hill, University of Nebraska Press/Potomac Books, Health Communications, Inc., AMG Publishers, and Press 53. In 2014, Rodgers was named a Distinguished Alumna from Tarrant County College/NE Campus. Three of her aviation poems from the book Because I Fly (McGraw-Hill) were featured in an exhibit at the Cradle of Aviation Museum on Long Island, NY. In 2017, the Clovis Municipal School Foundation in Clovis, NM awarded her the Purple Pride Hall of Honor Award under the "Sports and Entertainment" category.

"Johnnie Come Lately" first released from Camel Press in paperback & e-book in 2015. In 2018, Thorndike Press, the leading large print publisher in the United States, released "Johnnie Come Lately" and the sequel, "Seven Wings to Glory," in hardcover large print library binding. One of Kathleen's goals as a novelist is to shine the spotlight on military families through the art of storytelling.

In the excerpt below, Johnnie Kitchen, a forty-three-year-old wife and mother of three, pens a journal entry to her late father, a man she only met once when she was a young girl. He was KIA in Vietnam November 22, 1970.

Johnnie's Journal

Memorial Day

May 28, 2007

Dear Father "Unknown":

At least that's what my birth certificate says about you. Mama's name appears as a statement next to the word Mother: Victoria Grubbs. No question about it. But not Father. You appear as one eyebrow-raising word: UNKNOWN. But I guess unknown is better than nothing at all. Better than a flatline _____ after the word "father." As if you've always been dead.

Until Dale found those two photos, you'd been like an unknown soldier to me: a vague recollection of a man in uniform. Today, on a day set aside to remember our war dead, my kids—your grandkids—finally have a face to go with your name and rank.

I hope you didn't suffer,

Johnnie

Kathleen M. Rodgers, author of *The Final Salute*, *Johnnie Come Lately*, and *Seven Wings to Glory*. She has recently completed her fourth novel and is represented by Diane Nine of Nine Speakers, Inc.

https://kathleenmrodgers.com

Part 1: War and Military Stories

CHARLIE VINROOT

AFLOAT WITH THE BLUE WATER NAVY TONKIN GULF 64-65

Those of us 'Nam Vets who didn't spend much, if any, time in country like the ground pounders and grunts did, spent a lot of time in the Gulf between Dixie Station (down South) and Yankee Station (up North near Hainan Island) where the conflict, police action, war (whatever you call it) began.

My career began with my LCDR (USNR) dad swearing me in on my 17th birthday. I was inducted in a 2X6 program, 2 years active duty 4 in the USNR. I was granted a deferment to complete high school and then 4 years of college. After that, I went to OCS.

Immediately after graduation from Officer Candidate School in Newport, Rhode Island, I received orders to report to USS INDEPENDENCE (CVA-62). And after a very short in port time and a short Air Wing workup at Sea, we departed for Vietnam around the Horn of Africa. I also learned that I was to be assigned as B Division Officer (Boilers). Luckily, I didn't know a damned thing about Steam Engineering (remember my BSEE (Electrical Engineering))! Fortunately, I had a CWO-4 Warrant Officer, by the name of Bob Ballinger who saved my young (22yo) ass. Bob later worked for me when I was an O-5 in Naval Sea Systems Command in Washington, D.C. and Technical Director of the Battleship Reactivation Program in 80-84, but that's another story entirely.

Anyhow, once reaching the Tonkin Gulf in very early 1965, we immediately joined in what had become an all-out conflict. We were usually 90 days "on the line" steaming 24 hours a day, launching aircraft 12 of those, usually, but at times all 24 hours with the 80 aircraft Carrier Air Wing 7 flying 12 on12 off. As a Junior Officer, I ate in the Dirty Shirt wardroom on the 03 level (right under the flight deck) and my bunk room with 5 other J.O.s wasn't too far away. Neither were the two bow catapults over our heads! The pilots ate in this wardroom in their flight suits which were a lot cleaner than my coveralls from the Holes (the Main Machinery rooms) in the hot deep bowels of the ship. I made friends with a few of them, but avoided doing so after of them didn't show up for any meals again.

Once in a while I was invited to dine with some of the Senior Officers the 2nd Deck, immediately under the Hangar Deck, which was 4 decks below my bunkroom and Dirty Shirt wardroom. One day while there, I was confronted by the Captain with a letter and a broad smile on his face. After opening the missive, I found that I had been directed to report for my Draft Physical 2 days before the letter was put in my hands. Apparently, it took them 4+ months to figure out I had graduated from college, but they had not yet discerned that I was on Active Duty with the USN. The Captain told me not to worry about it, but it was hard not to. He said he "would take care of it." He must have because I never heard from them again.

It was a difficult 11 months however, as we lost 14 pilots. A few were returned to the ship by rescue helos but most never did, being killed or captured or just plain MIA. Some were released when John McCain was when they returned the prisoners from the Hanoi Hilton.

I "augmented" into the USN shortly after I was promoted to Lt(jg), O-2. I could not become a regular line officer because of my eyesight. I was designated an Engineering Duty Officer.

This cruise was followed by a Med cruise, Graduate School in Monterey, many shore duty stations and one more Sea Tour on USS LUCE (DLG7/DDG38) in 73-75 as an O-4 Chief Engineer. I retired in late 1991, as an O-6 after 32 years of service.

Would I do it again, you're damn right! In a heartbeat...

Charlie Vinroot

Part 1: War and Military Stories

DWIGHT ZIMMERMAN

Dwight Zimmerman is an award winning author, a freelance writer and an editor. Dwight is an astute military historian and is a board member of the Military Writer's Society of America. (MWSA)

I am happy Dwight has provided this writing for us:

I was twelve years old when President Lyndon Johnson formally deployed American troops to South Vietnam in response to the Tonkin Gulf incident. My hometown was Devils Lake, North Dakota, population give-or-take 7,000. My home state was rural, economy based on agriculture, located in the middle of the continent and it had a population then of around 700,000. But for the neighboring states, no one in the country knew or cared about North Dakota—assuming they could even locate it on a map. But thanks to two Air Force Strategic Air Command bases (one at Grand Forks, 92 miles east, and the other at Minot, 95 miles to the west) and more than 100 Minuteman nuclear missile silos scattered about the state, the Russians knew where we were!

During my first three years of primary school at Minnie H, I remember participating in periodic hide-under-the-desk nuclear attack drills. And there were those black and orange nuclear fallout shelter signs affixed to various buildings, one of them being the implement dealership building where my dad worked. Occasionally we'd hear that hollow double-tap of a sonic boom, letting us know that somewhere high overhead a military fighter was flying faster than the speed of sound. Most indelible was the one day in which a B-52 bomber buzzed the town. First there was this deafening roar of its jet engines and then we saw it—the bomber flying low overhead almost filling the sky.

Back then, television viewing was limited to three networks NBC, CBS, and the upstart ABC, a couple of independent stations that aired old movies and syndicated programs, and a PBS station. Network news programs were thirty minutes long. NBC's anchors were the team of Chet Huntley and David Brinkley whose signature sign-off was "Goodnight, David." "Goodnight, Chet." ABC had Peter Jennings, but the most memorable of them belonged to CBS, Walter Cronkite. So great was his influence that he was known as "Uncle Walter."

KXJB based in Fargo was the CBS affiliate and my family's go-to station for television news. From 1965 on and with rare exception, Uncle Walter's lead story was something about what was happening in Vietnam, and he regularly led that segment with the latest body-count figure of enemy troops killed provided by the Defense Department. I remember that it struck me odd back then, like it was some sort of morbid score.

Like just about everyone else in the country, I knew nothing about Vietnam or its location before it began appearing on television news. But, once troops were on the ground in force, it became a nightly news item. And, as time passed, a baffling one for me.

My father had served in the Army during World War II. I was a huge fan of World War II history, reading every book in the library about it and buying the Ballantine Books paperbacks on the subject that were being released at the time. In that war, we and our allies were the good guys. After some years of hard fighting, we defeated the bad guys—attacking them in lands they had conquered and then in their homeland.

With Vietnam we were told that the communist North Vietnamese were the bad guys and that we were there to help keep the democratic good-guy South Vietnamese free from communism.

But, then why were Buddhist monks in South Vietnam pouring gasoline over themselves and then setting themselves on fire in suicidal protest over their government? And why did we seem to keep repeatedly fight over the same sections of South Vietnamese territory? And, since we knew the North Vietnamese was using a supply route they carved out in neighboring Laos and Cambodia called the Ho Chi Minh Trail to run supplies to its troops in the south, why didn't we attack that supply line and cut it off? And, why didn't we invade North Vietnam and end the threat entirely?

Truth to tell, for most of those years, I didn't pay too much attention to what was going on in Vietnam and what it might mean to me. It was there in the background, but certainly not influencing my school life. That started to change in 1968. That year was a very bad one for our country. It began with the communist Tet Offensive that shocked everyone in America, followed by nationwide civil rights and anti-war riots and protests, President Johnson announcing he would not seek re-election, the assassinations of Dr. Martin Luther King and Democratic presidential hopeful Robert F. Kennedy (whose brother President John F. Kennedy had also been assassinated), the chaotic Democratic National Convention in Chicago—even in such a faraway state as North Dakota we felt like the nation was falling apart. But what particularly captured my attention was the sight of male college students in anti-war protests burning their draft cards.

Conscription was a law of the land back then and every high school male once he turned seventeen years old had to register for what was popularly called "the Draft." Once a year a Draft lottery was held in which days of the month were selected. The unofficial rule of thumb was that those who found their birth dates landing in the first third, roughly numbers 1-130, might as well volunteer as that group was guaranteed to be drafted. Those in the second group, roughly 131-260, were fence-sitters. If the nation was at war, their chances of being drafted were strong. If not, less so. Those who wound up in the last third, roughly 261-365, could basically consider themselves low-risk and unlikely to be drafted unless we were in a conflict like World War II.

With the war in Vietnam escalating, but seeming to go at best nowhere and at worse downhill, and with young men returning from that war in numbers and telling harrowing stories of what it was like and being the brunt of anti-war protests, which were becoming more numerous and violent, I found myself becoming more and more confused and worried. Basically, everything revolved around this one question: If we are in a war, why aren't we in it, to win it? Nothing was making sense about us being there.

I had bad eyesight but didn't know if it was bad enough to render me unfit for military service. I began reading what I could about what to expect in the military, which in those pre-Internet days wasn't much. I began considering my options. I had heard about protesters who emigrated to Canada and Sweden, but

I didn't like that idea. I believe it was in 1970, my junior year in high school, that President Richard Nixon announced that no draftees would be sent to Vietnam. I didn't quite trust that statement. I decided that if my number came up, I'd avoid the Army and look to volunteer in one of the other services.

I don't remember on what day my draft year lottery was held. But I do remember reading the newspaper the following day to see where my birth date, June 2, fell. In that list was an answer that would affect my life one way or another. As my eyes began scanning down the list, I found myself going deeper and deeper into it, past that "magic" number of 130, then the other magic number of 260. Finally, five numbers before the end, there it was: June 2: 360. Too many years have passed for me to remember how I outwardly reacted. I only remember that I felt relieved.

As it turned out, I didn't go into uniform. My future eventually had me writing about those who did, and to try and explain why we fought the Vietnam War.

Dwight Jon Zimmerman, New York Times Best Selling Author

Artwork: Trieu Hoang

DUKE BARRETT

Duke Barrett is a Vietnam War Veteran. Duke has authored "The Wall of Broken Dreams," which may be purchased through his website. Duke has provided this writing for us today:

A Few Memories of my First Days In Country

I had arrived fresh out of jump school with a plane load of other newly minted paratroopers on a Continental Airlines 707 jet Plane from Travis Air Force base Ca, to Tan Son Khut Air Base, Saigon, South Vietnam. Shortly after touchdown we were taken to the 90th Replacement Camp, a.k.a. Camp Alpha, to await our assignments, or better said, our fate, but not before we were mustered in and out of the host country air terminal at the base.

Culture shock greeted us immediately at our point of arrival as we disembarked our first class like flight to our third world destination. Our senses were immediately attacked by the unrelenting heat and humidity of the land, foreign to most of us for sure. Once inside the terminal, the attack continued with foreign odors of food and tobacco permeating the air, the native spoken tongue and not to mention the unconventional restroom facilities, again, alien to us. Suffice it to say that this introduction set us Yanks aback and I believe it was at that point our involuntary assimilation to Southeast Asia had just begun.

Immediately following our comfort break we were whisked off the tarmac by a few army buses and transported to our temporary housing facilities at Camp Alpha, adjacent to the Tan Son Khut Airbase. Now, up to this point army housing had been anything but comfortable but our new accommodations were even less so than the traditional army quarters we'd had become accustomed to in our short military careers. Our new digs were noisy, really noisy, situated only meters from a runway that mission bound F-4 Phantom's used 24 hours a day.

Our shelter was also incredibly hot; screened and sand bagged walls with a roof of corrugated tin making the evening rain sound something like the "end of the world" to those of us who'd never experienced life under tin roofs. In days to come I longed for the privilege of living under tin again.

Duke Barret, 1/8 Cav (abn) 1st Air Cav Div.

Norm Kober

Norm Kober, another Vietnam War Veteran, and I went to the same high school back in the day. We reconnected several years ago through my writing. Norm is a successful upper level manager for the Chik a-fil restaurant chain where he travels extensively holding various seminars. He has been back to Vietnam several times on good will trips for his company. Norm has shared these thoughts for our article.

The Vietnam War was a waste for everyone, all three sides lost in more ways than we can count. The North did achieve victory in the war, but they never captured the hearts of the people of the south. The people all over Vietnam both north and south want the same things Americans want, that's freedom to make a life for our families and ourselves that is improving and satisfying, where we can worship without fear, and with hope that our children and grandchildren will be able to do the same. My Life was changed forever because of Vietnam, the first two times I was there as an airman in the service of my country, I fixed aircraft and loaded wounded and dead soldiers on transport planes to leave the country, I grew up in many ways, some I don't talk about because of shame, and some I can say I'm proud of. The last two times I visited Vietnam I went in service to mankind to help make someone's life better. I grew more on the last two trips then the first two. I learned that you can't win a war with a gun, you can win battles for territory with weapons but you won't win the love, honor, and respect of people if your shooting at their countryman.

Norm Kober

THE CRITTERS OF VIETNAM

Upon being surprised by a predator in the wild, your memory is seared for life.

Joe

Anyone who knows a Vietnam War veteran has probably heard many stories about the wildlife they encountered during their tour of duty. My friend and fellow author, Vietnam Veteran John Podlaski recently added a story to his website about the critters of the Nam. This is my recollection on the subject.

Vietnam, a beautiful country that even at war, teemed with wildlife.

Vietnam is a tropical country on the edge of a large continent, bordered by an ocean. It has a diverse topography along with many flowing rivers and streams. And there are critters…many critters.

One thing that constantly amazed me during my tour of duty in Vietnam was the number of critters that were able to survive in that deadly war torn environment. Back home; you crack a twig and every deer within earshot takes off like a rocket. Somehow the wildlife in Vietnam managed to survive, and in some cases thrive, while tens of thousands of firefights, bombing sorties, naval bombardments, artillery missions and chemical defoliations took place. How did they manage?

The place was noisy—very noisy… and dangerous… nonstop. Yet tigers, leopards, vast troops of monkeys, elephants, too many snakes to mention and even rhinoceroses survived in that toxic environment. It wasn't surprising that the insects survived... they're designed to survive under any condition. And hordes of insects occupied Vietnam. Immense rice beetles, mounds of stinging ants, scorpions, spiders of every make and model....and of course the mosquitoes that tortured every GI who ever set foot in-country.

Those mosquitoes, ever present day or night, rain or shine; would swoop down in hordes getting into your mouth, nose, eyes, and ears. The military doled out mosquito repellent that could strip paint, but it barely slowed them down. After a month or two you just took them in stride. Of course the grunts in the bush all day had it the worst; but the mosquitoes spared no one because of rank or station.

My experiences with the "critters of the Nam" are similar to others who served during the war. Although to this day I am not overly pestered by mosquitoes, they certainly cramped my style in Vietnam. Sleeping was the worst. Some guys obtained mosquito netting to put around their bunks. I found the netting to be very bothersome. (Besides, someone stole mine.)

All the hooches, barracks and buildings on the Phu Cat airbase were occupied by hordes of large hairy spiders. They looked like a small tarantula and were everywhere. I waged war on them constantly, dispersing the deadly Military grade insect repellent like Agent Orange. It didn't put much of a dent in their population; but I wasn't going to let them roll me over.

Rats were another problem. HUGE rats. They also occupied most buildings and structures everywhere. One ran over my chest one night when I was laying in my bunk. No sleep that night. Always short of protein, the ever practical Vietnamese put them on the menu. (Another reason I never dined with them)

Many American GIs made pets out of the local monkeys. They looked cute, but most of them were meaner than a mother-in-law without a grandchild. They would savagely bite anything other than themselves and I avoided them like the Vietnamese put them on the menu. (Another reason I never dined with them)

Cobras preyed on the huge rats that ran amok.

Snakes were ever present in Vietnam. Cobras were frequently found on base and shot on sight. In one incident, I witnessed a hapless perimeter guard trying to shoot a cobra that was approaching him aggressively. He kept trying to shoot the snakes head, but the snake, dodging like Muhammad Ali, kept right on coming. Finally a well-seasoned guard casually approached the snake and lopped off it's head with a small machete.

Our hooch dog "Noah," a feral dog we had adopted, became an overnight hero because of a cobra. He had supposedly killed one that had entered the barracks one night, and was heaped with lavish praise. It has always been my opinion that Noah found a dead cobra and dragged it into the barracks to eat—but I wasn't going to rain on his parade. Good for Noah.

Another snake of note was the Southeast Asian pit viper. A small snake of various colors it was referred to as a "two-stepper" because supposedly once it bit someone they took two steps and dropped dead. This snake was more of a problem for the Vietnamese who wore only sandals or nothing at all on their feet. American GIs with their heavily canvased jungle boots were protected from any bites to their feet or ankles.

The "two stepper" terminated many Vietnamese.

The Phu Cat airbase had a large "open" area which was occupied by many creatures—some four legged, some two. A leopard from the area appeared one day and got itself backed into a storage bay at an outside warehousing area. People tried to drive it away but it just sat their snarling and screaming. I was able to see it, and the ferociousness of it certainly made an impression on me. Unfortunately it had to be shot, after which many GIs posed for pictures with it.

Another animal I saw, right on the Phu Cat airbase, made a lifelong impression on me. Three of us were walking down a small road, heading back to our hooch one evening around dusk. A jeep came along and we made way so it could pass. Soon we saw the jeep stop for a few minutes. Then it backed up all the way to us. The jeep driver told us to get in. We thanked him but said we'd rather walk. Since he was very insistent we got in and he drove to the spot where he had stopped a minute before.

Leopards occasionally preyed on the villagers.

There, hunkered down in some thick brush sat a tiger. With a low growling it sat glaring at us. We watched it for several minutes. The driver wanted to drive it off so it wouldn't ambush anyone. (There were at least eight confirmed cases of American GI fatalities during the war as a result of tiger attacks.)

Though beautiful, tigers were a threat to Vietnamese and Americans alike.

The driver leaned on the horn of the jeep, after which the tiger let out a blood curdling roar and then quietly backed off and slipped into the night. We reported the incident to the Apes (air police) who casually brushed it off. They said there were a couple of tigers that traveled on and off of the base all the time, and if they shot it another would just take its place. I was glad that no one came to harm that night, us or the tiger. It was a beautiful animal.

The critter incident I had in Vietnam which created the most grief for me personally, involved ants. The ants in Vietnam swarmed like bees, and bit like mules. They were worse than the mosquitoes. At Christmas time my Mother sent me a goody package. In it was a small tinned ham. My two buddies and I quickly devoured half of it, after which I left for about fifteen minutes to attend to something. When I returned, the ham was a living mound of ants, about twice the size of the ham itself. I cussed and roared and dispersed the ants with fire, but alas ... the ham was ruined. I groused about that for at least a week, and harbor it to this day!

Weapons of the Vietnam War

Every gun that is made, every warship launched, every rocket fired signifies in the final sense, a theft from those who hunger and are not fed, those who are cold and are not clothed. This world in arms is not spending money alone. It is spending the sweat of its laborers, the genius of its scientists, the hopes of its children. This is not a way of life at all in any true sense. Under the clouds of war, it is humanity hanging on a cross of iron.

Dwight D. Eisenhower

Some of the more memorable weapons of the Vietnam War

The Huey, perhaps the most familiar image of the Vietnam War.

The Vietnam War (the American War in Vietnam) ran on for many years. Primarily a guerrilla type war, weapons of many kinds were employed by all belligerent parties during the long struggle in Southeast Asia. Though not intended to be all encompassing, this article will discuss some of the more familiar weapons of the war, as well as some of the more unusual weaponry employed during that time, and some controversial weapons used as well.

After all these years, many people, veterans and civilians alike, are familiar with the most common types of weaponry employed in the Vietnam War theater. The iconic Huey helicopter, aka the workhorse of Vietnam, is certainly one of the most familiar weapon systems of the war. As a matter of fact, one of the Facebook groups I belong to is dedicated to helicopters of the Vietnam War, and of course the Huey is a main topic.

M-16 variants

The M-16 rifle is another weapon highly associated with the Vietnam War. In the mid-sixties the M-16 replaced the M-14 as the standard infantry weapon of the war. When I arrived at my base in Vietnam, I was given a brand-new M-16. The first thing I did was tear it down, and a good thing. The firing pin had a hairline crack in it. I was given another M-16, not brand new, but with no defects. As an airman who spent much of my time on the airbase, I didn't rely on the weapon nearly as much as my less fortunate brothers in the Army and Marine infantry, who spent most of their time out in the bush. Much maligned in the early stages of it's release the M-16 was eventually debugged, is still around to this day, and has lent itself to many different variations of the weapon.

Another iconic weapon of the Vietnam War, and still in use, is the United States Air Force B-52 strategic bomber. "Buff" as it is known, flew many missions over the skies of Vietnam during the war, both north and south. The huge aircraft was stationed at bases in Thailand and Guam, where they had ample runway space for take off and landing. The area adjoining our Phu Cat airbase was bombed many times during my tour, and frequently it was done by B-52's. It was quite an earth-shattering occasion when they did, because first you would hear a rumbling growing louder and louder, then you would hear explosions and finally, if they were close enough you would feel the shock waves. Seldom could we see the aircraft, high in the sky or hidden behind cloud cover. Whenever the B-52 bombings occurred I always felt bad for anyone who might have been on the receiving end of those bombardments, friend or enemy. After the war, many North Vietnamese soldiers, civilians, and Vietcong alike, stated that the B-52 Bomber was the most feared weapon of the war.

Part 1: War and Military Stories

The most feared weapon of the war.

The United States Naval gun boat was also a weapon of note during the war. The brown water Navy conducted operations with small gun boats throughout the Vietnam War, in both coastal and inland waters. Their mission ranged from interdiction and aid as well as search and rescue sometimes of ground forces or pilots who were in trouble out in the bush. Heavily armed and fast, these boats were very efficient at their given tasks.

We must also include the U.S. Navy aircraft carrier among those stalwart weapons systems of the Vietnam War. Many missions, in both North and South Vietnam were conducted by aircraft off of those vessels.

Any discussion regarding weapons of the Vietnam War would be incomplete without including those employed, very affectively in many cases, by the Vietcong and the North Vietnamese Army (NVA). The AK-47 rifle, still very much in use to this day throughout the world, was carried by communist forces, both north and south. Surface to air (SAM) missiles were effectively used by North Vietnam against attacking B-52 bombers and other aircraft. And since one cost me the hearing in my right ear, I cannot omit the 122MM rocket from this conversation. The Vietcong (VC) used it very effectively, along with mortars, to bombard American facilities throughout the war.

There are many other weapons systems, large and small that bring back memories of our time in Vietnam. What branch we served in, where in Vietnam we served, and also when we served in Vietnam makes a difference, in many cases, in which weapons systems most strikes our memory.

And some unconventional weapons of the Vietnam War

During the course of the long war, many different conditions and problems arose, regarding the nature of the battle at hand. Over time, both sides of the conflict introduced a considerable variety of weaponry which they felt was necessary to address those challenges. The US Air Force, Navy, Army and Marines used many different types of aircraft in the conflict. Some, like the C-47 Gooney Bird, and the B-26 Marauder dated back to WWII.

Surprising, but very effective air frames, were the Cessna O-1, O-2 and the OV-10 Bronco. These aircraft were used in Forward Air Control (FAC) and also in reconnaissance and rescue missions. Some were equipped with armament, not only to defend themselves, but also in an offensive capacity, depending on the mission.

Above: FAC driver's had guts! Below: The business end of an AC-47 gunship.

As an "assistant loadmaster" for a short time I loaded, unloaded and traveled on three different types of aircraft throughout the Central Highlands of South Vietnam. And each of those had armed versions which were very lethal. The AC-130 gunships replaced AC-47 gunships (Spooky) as the low altitude attack gunship during the war. AC-119s, were also used in that capacity. All three were deadly and much feared by the enemy.

One of the most unusual weapons of war employed in a modern conflict was the bow and arrow. Special Forces units used the long bow, as well as the Montagnard crossbow as needed, primarily where stealth and silence were critical. The Montagnard crossbow, though not impressive to look at, was quite lethal and could pierce through a protective flack vest.

L-R: Special Forces trooper with long bow and Montagnard (Yard) with crossbow

The Vietcong also employed a wide array of unique weapons throughout the war. Not able to keep up with American technology, they often employed booby traps, such as the punji trap and variations of it. Photos of this, and some similar anti-personnel weapons are included with this article. The VC also possessed a unique, though primitive anti-tank weapon as well as an anti-helicopter weapon. Always stretched for resources, the Vietcong also relied on weaponry recovered from battles, as well as weapons acquired through the black market which thrived during the Vietnam War. Through this process they acquired many U.S. weapons, such as the M-16 rifle.

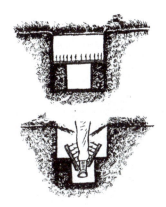
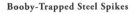
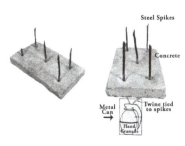
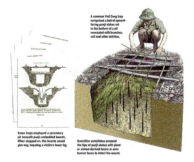

Vietcong anti-personnel weaponry

Controversy

It would be impossible to review the history of any war and not find issues which created controversy. The treatment of prisoners during the civil war, by both North and South, mustard gas in WWI, concentration camps and fire bombing in WWII, are some examples of such controversy. And as such, by its nature, the Vietnam War has also produced controversies. It is not the author's intent to level judgment regarding the issue, only to communicate information.

Napalm, a petroleum product manufactured in jell form and released from aircraft, caused horrific injuries and suffering. The practice of burning "enemy" huts by some American forces was also a contentious activity.

Part 1: War and Military Stories

The VC often used terrorism to spread fear.

Acts of terrorism by the Vietcong were brutal in nature and questionable regarding their effectiveness, as they were primarily used against civilians who they were supposedly trying to help.

The brutalization of American prisoners of war in North Vietnam was also a type of weapon of terrorism, designed to strike fear and misgivings into their enemies. The stalwart men imprisoned, however, proved to be a match for all of the torture inflicted upon them. The bravest of the brave.

The sad legacy of Agent Orange remains

Agent Orange, the herbicide defoliant developed by Monsanto, was and still is, the most controversial weapon of the war. Intended to be used to deny the enemy cover, the chemical has now been attributed to many serious health conditions, with many Vietnam War Veterans still suffering and dying from it's use. Moreover, the Vietnamese are heavily impacted as well, as the toxic chemical remains embedded in the soil and waterways where it was originally dispersed. Having been directly affected by Agent Orange, I am acutely aware of the issues at hand.

Perhaps some day we won't need them.

The weapons of war, though perhaps not a topic for dinner party conversation, are of immense interest to those of us who wish to understand the field of war and the weaponries so employed. For most, it is our hope and desire, that these tools of death and suffering not be needed or used, however until that day comes, we must be cognizant of all weapons of war, be they used for good…or evil.

Flying the Friendly Skies of Vietnam

(Published in The Kenosha News, 1/26/2020)

If you expected everything to make sense, you were soon disappointed.

Joe

Scrounging for Parts in a Two Hundred Billion Dollar War

Vietnamization marked the end of Americanization

For almost one month during my fun filled, all-expense paid visit to Vietnam in 1970, I was a member of an aircrew.

President Richard Nixon's program of Vietnamization was in full swing, and things were rapidly changing. The program was an attempt to extricate the U.S. by turning the war over to the South Vietnamese military, in full. And the very first day the program was signed, military supplies and equipment for the unpopular war began to dry up. Of course, the South Vietnamese were nowhere near being prepared for the hand-off, so the American forces at hand had to continue all of their missions, albeit with fewer supplies and equipment.

Assigned to various functions in supply, I spent most of my time at or near the Phu Cat airbase in the Central Highlands of Vietnam. Scrambling for supplies and equipment was a way of life, but soon after Nixon's program unfolded, we came in dire need of many additional items just to keep the birds flying…and the Vietcong at bay. One of the first airbases to shutdown was Nha Trang, a few hundred miles south of Phu Cat. In addition to being an airbase, Nha Trang was home to a large Special Forces operation. Around September of 1970, I was sent to Nha Trang to scrounge any materials which they may have had, that we were in need of at Phu Cat.

Though still under communist control, today's Nha Trang is a vacation destination

I was looking forward to the detail, I thought it would be a piece of cake. But as with most things in the war, it turned out to be anything but that. Nha Trang, an in-country R & R center, was right on the coast of Vietnam and was famous for it's beautiful white sand beaches. Armed with only a pile of paper work, I hopped on a C-130 Hercules and landed at Nha Trang several hours later, eager to carry out my mission.

THE BEST LAID PLANS OF MEN & MICE

The supply warehouse at Nha Trang was a disaster

Upon my arrival at Nha Trang, I headed right over to the supply warehouse, to lay claim to the materials that Phu Cat needed. When I arrived at the warehouse, I was surprised to see a long line of both air force and army personnel sent as scavengers from military posts all over South Vietnam. That's when I realized this wasn't going to be as easy as I had thought.

The airmen assigned to the warehouse had been worked to a frazzle, they were spread thin...and in foul humor. Realizing I would not be able to submit my material request until at least the next day, I went through the warehouse, looking for the materials needed at Phu Cat. I hoped to find and mark them so they could be readily identified and shipped off asap. Surprised again, I found none of the supplies and equipment on my list. I got in line once more, and when it was my turn to submit my requirements, I was told to just leave my report and come back the next day. With nothing else to do, I found my quarters, and then took a nice swim in the South China Sea. It was wonderful. I also found a Red Cross center, occupied by two American donut dollies. Not having seen any Western women for quite some time, I hung around their compound like a love struck school boy.

Even at war, the beaches of Nha Trang were beautiful.

The next couple of days were spent trying to wrangle the needed materials from members of the other U.S. military facilities who had shown up looking for goods. Most were disappointed at what was available at Nha Trang and full-scale bartering and trading activities ensued. As it turned out, few if any had anything, we were in need of at Phu Cat, and many were short of the same items we were. The best I could do was leave my list of requirements with the ill-humored on-site staff, who said they would look at it at some time in the future and ship whatever they could find. True to their word, they eventually sent a large amount of materials and equipment to Phu Cat, unfortunately it was surplus junk they didn't want to deal with at Nha Trang, not what we needed or requested. So, the whole detail turned into a bungled mess ... what we in the military called a clusterf..k. (Kind of like the whole damn war)

SHANGHAIED

The C-130, the workhorse of the U.S.A.F. in Vietnam

Packed up and ready to head back to Phu Cat on the third or fourth day, I was stopped on the flight line by an Air Force officer. "Campo is it?" He asked, trying to read my nametag. "Campolo, sir," I replied. He looked me over and ordered me to head back into the small Nha Trang air terminal.

Damn, what the hell did I do now? I wondered.

As it turned out, the officer, a major, had no issue with anything I had done, he just needed another body to load cargo aircraft for the next couple of weeks. (A beefy guy, wide in the back with a distinctive brow ridge, apparently) He explained that I would load and unload any and everything at each base or airfield on designated flight routes. He officially dubbed me an "assistant load-master." (In other words, a pack mule.) When I put up concerns, he assured me he would contact my superiors at Phu Cat and let them know I would be unavailable for a short time. He sweetened the pot by guaranteeing me flight pay for three months-time. That along with my regular pay and the hazardous duty pay I was already receiving for being in Nam, translated into a nice round figure. Now he had my interest. Most of the money we made over there was put into bank accounts for us, as there wasn't any place to spend much of it anyway. I was building up a nice fat nest egg. And apparently I wasn't as invaluable as I thought, because no one from Phu Cat put up a fuss over my abduction by the Major.

So, the next three weeks found me flying around the Central Highlands of South Vietnam, loading and unloading aircraft. It was almost one month before the major released me and I was able to return to Phu Cat.

See the War in Nam in your Cargo plane

As with the C-130 & C-47, the C-119 had a very lethal armed version.

The first aircraft I was assigned to on these missions was the Lockheed C-130 Hercules, an aircraft I was already familiar with, having traveled on one over much of the Central Highlands of South Vietnam at one time or another. But loading and unloading the aircraft brought me a new appreciation for this beast of burden. We'd load pallets of goods on the ground, then roll them up the reclining back gate and strap them in. Unloading was much quicker, of course, especially those instances when we dropped pallets of goods while still in the air. When this occurred, it was done at low altitude and speed, because the landing strip was too short, compromised or under attack. We also transported troops, Vietnamese civilians and their livestock on occasion. Whenever we transported livestock, the interior would require a good hosing down, as pigs, sheep and chickens did not enjoy flying. (Nor did some of those tending them.)

The C-123 was also used to distribute the deadly toxin Agent Orange

I mostly lived on these aircraft for three- and one-half weeks, and the least favorite aircraft of which I was assigned to was the Fairchild C-119. The "flying boxcar", as it was called, dated back to pre-Korean War days, and was loaded from the rear also. Smaller than the C-130, and less durable, the aircraft held no charm for me.

One of the missions I went out on was on a C-123 Provider. Also built by Fairchild, the C-123, infamous for dispersing the lethal toxin Agent Orange throughout the war, was the smallest aircraft I flew on. Flying out of Pleiku, the mission was a resupply effort for the Marine outpost at Dak To. The outpost had been under attack on and off and though our landing was uncertain, we made it in, rubber side down, and got out of there in a damn hurry! Not a fun trip.

Several of my flying days were spent on a Douglass C-47 Skytrain. This was my favorite aircraft by far. Notable as the WWII paratrooper carrier, it was another durable vessel capable of flying under many adverse conditions. Most of the duty on this aircraft involved moving people; troops, civilians or both. We always left the jump door open, and took turns sitting on the floor, hanging onto the webbing with our legs dangling out. From the air, Vietnam was a beautiful country and those flights on the C-47's, legs dangling in the wind, lost in my thoughts, was to be the most pleasant of all my time in Vietnam.

The deadly armed version of the C-47

The flight crews on all of these aircraft had my admiration. Up and down, day and night through all kinds of weather and conditions. And although the Vietcong had no air force, and the North Vietnamese knew better than to send it's Russian Migs up against the formidable American flying machines, the VC still managed to cause problems. They would sit off the end of the runways and shoot at the planes landing and taking off, usually with recoilless rifles or AK-47's. To counter that threat, the ascents and descents from all of these airfields and bases were very steep.

The pilot and co-pilots carried their own "butt plates" with them. These were steel plates, formed in the shape of the human seat, which placed over the aircraft seat offered the crews protection from ground fire. It was a bit humorous, watching senior officers carrying this comical looking device around with them, but it no doubt saved a lot of lives and injuries. Weather was also a considerable factor in the Southeast Asian theater. Fog, heavy cloud cover and monsoon rains made for some treacherous flying, and many aircraft in the conflict were lost as a result of it. The Central Highlands of South Vietnam was loaded with mountain ranges, so that hazard was added to the mix. I cannot say enough about the courage and dedication of all of the flight crews who dealt with these conditions on a day to day basis.

A FLIGHT TO REMEMBER

Pleiku Airbase was a welcome site after our aircraft was hit.

My last flight assignment during this time, was on another C-130, and it was a memorable one. The loadmaster and I had worked together for a couple of days on the same aircraft. Loaded up and headed down the runway, we took our usual seats in the far back, opposite of each other. There was an old parachute on one of the seats, that we hardly took notice of, up until that point. Flying out of Pleiku airbase, we left around mid-afternoon. As usual, the ascent was steep, but not as steep as needed, evidently, because we were soon hit by ground fire from a Vietcong recoilless rifle. The round hit the C-130 in the tail section, and for a moment the aircraft shuddered like a dog in the rain.

A bit stunned, the loadmaster and I looked at each other, then at a small hole below the tail section which was clearly visible. The wind now whistled through the hole, canceling out the usual noise and racket the large aircraft made. As if on cue, we both looked at the lone parachute sitting on the webbed seat, and then at each other with a blank stare. (Who would get it?)

Almost immediately one of the pilots came down from the cockpit, walked back and inspected the damage hole. He made a couple of comments about it not really being a "big deal," made a hand gesture indicating he was not impressed, and walked back to the front of the aircraft. We watched him a bit anxiously as he climbed back up to the cockpit.

Soon, we felt the aircraft turning around and descending in altitude. In just a short time, we landed back at Pleiku, where a couple of emergency vehicles waited on the runway. They were not necessary, however, as the minor damage to the tail did not affect the operational capability of the stalwart C-130 in the least.

Our nerves, however, were definitely affected and we exited the aircraft on wobbly legs. The damage to the tail section was visibly evident, but not really that bad considering the hit it had taken. The loadmaster and I were given a couple of days off, and the major back at Nha Trang, upon hearing of the incident, allowed me to return to Phu Cat to resume my normal duties. The Air Force did me a good turn by continuing my flight pay for several more months, well into my next duty station at March Air Force base in Riverside, California, even though I no longer flew on any missions. In my second month of duty at March Air Force base, I was given the opportunity to fly to Hawaii and stay for a week—if I agreed to act in my old capacity as an "assistant loadmaster." (Mule again!) Not wanting to pass up a free trip to Hawaii, I agreed to go. The aircraft turned out to be another C-119 flying boxcar, which I disliked—but I had a great time in Hawaii. On the return trip, the last item I off loaded from the C-119 was a surfboard I had paid twenty dollars for in Honolulu. (I always was a scrounger.)

Those were the last of my flying days with the U.S. Air Force. Manure clean-up, shootings and sick passengers aside, I thoroughly enjoyed the duty. And Phu Cat airbase was turned over to the South Vietnamese just one year after I left.

In 1975, it fell to the North Vietnamese Army.

THE AGE OF AQUARIUS

(Published in Happenings Magazine SmartReader 1/28/2021)

War is a ferocious form of insanity.

Corra May Harris

I served in the United States Air Force from 1968 to 1972. I served in Vietnam from January 1970 to January 1971. I entered Vietnam as an Airman First Class (E-3) and left as a Staff Sergeant (E-5). I was stationed at Phu Cat Airbase in Binh Dinh Province in the Central Highlands of Vietnam, in what was designated as the 2 Corps military region. I was assigned to supply and my duties included warehouse work, running materials to and from other military facilities in the area—and for a little over one month, flying as a crew member on C-130, C-119 or C-47 aircraft, humping cargo.

The village of Phu Cat sat on the southern end of the air base, the rest of the base being surrounded by dense field or vegetation. The volatile province of Binh Dinh, Vietnam was never pacified and accounted for the fifth highest casualty rate for U.S. troops during the war, with upwards of seventy percent of the population estimated to be Viet Cong or Viet Cong sympathizers. The hootches we were quartered in consisted of half screen and half one inch plank structures. Each hootch at Phu Cat was surrounded by a 4 foot high, three foot thick sand bunker offering a degree of protection from shrapnel, incoming mortars, rockets and small arms fire.

Part 1: War and Military Stories

Our perimeter at Phu Cat—clean as a whistle thanks to agent orange. After the sun went down all hell broke loose.

At night our perimeter would come alive with small arms fire, mortar detonations and air-to-ground fire raging from sundown till sunup. Our hootch was very close to the perimeter and as a result we were in close proximity to much of the night-time action. When not on duty, one of our favorite activities was to sit on the sand bunkers, drinking, smoking and watching the evening fireworks. We would rate the action by intensity and shout and cheer at particularly heavy action. Occasionally, when the fighting was too intense or got too close, we would be forced to retreat behind the bunkers.

On one particular evening, the fighting was as crazy as we ever saw it. A firefight raged up and down the perimeter like a snake, and lasted for hours. Spooky and Puff gunships joined in, raining fire down from the sky as the battle intensified.

One crazy guy who hung with us, a zany character from New England named McCormick, often joined us during these shows. "Mac" was a tall, lanky good natured dude. He was always joking around, had a keen wit and a great fondness for gin and tonics. In Vietnam, we would often get shipments of alcohol of one kind or another by lot. For about four months while I was there, we got mostly gin, so naturally that's what we drank. We made our own tonic using quinine from the dispensary and white soda which we traded for. Mac was by far the leading consumer of our gin and tonics, notable for having drank thirty two on one particular evening alone.

On this particular night, Mac sat with us, drinking our gin and tonics, and watching the fighting rage on. Finally, the battle became too intense, forcing us to retreat behind the bunkers into the hootch. Undaunted by the intensity of the violence, Mac dragged out a speaker from a stereo in the hootch. He placed the speaker on top of the sand bunker, put a tape on the reel to reel inside the hootch, and turned the volume up full. Soon, amidst the explosions, shooting and screaming, "The Age of Aquarius," by The 5th Dimension blasted from the lone speaker sitting on the bunker.

It was a wild, surreal scene. We laughed, yelled and sang along with the peace anthem favorite, as the violence raged on.

And although I was to witness many unfortunate events in Vietnam, that event, though not tragic, remains one of the most memorable for me. To this day, I can still see Mac, hunkered down behind the bunker, gin and tonic in hand, flashing his patented evil grin.

The Stump Gang

(Published in Happenings Magazine SmartReader 2/25/2021)

The most important thing about a problem is not it's solution, but the strength we gain in finding the solution.

Seneca

In 1971, after two and a half years of military service, including one year in Vietnam, I landed a pretty cushy gig at March Air Force Base in Riverside, California. There, I would finish the remainder of my four-year Air Force commitment.

Now a Staff Sergeant, I was given a desk job in an air-conditioned office—filled with women no less! And as an E-5, I would soon be paid to live off base in the quarters of my choosing. (Within the compensated budget.)

Southern California was great duty, with access to the mountains, the desert, the Pacific Ocean, Las Vegas and Mexico. There was never any shortage of nifty places to visit.

Before I moved off base, I lived in the barracks for several months, with all of the highlights (and lowlights) that barracks life entails. Inspections, loud neighbors, boisterous parties, and the occasional brawl.

Our barracks was conveniently located right across the street from the NCO (Non-commissioned Officer) club and pool. That worked out great for those of us who liked to take a swim and have a refreshment or two after our daily duties were complete.

However, things were not as smooth as they could have been. During the late sixties and early seventies, the U.S. military was reeling from the double-edged sword of the Vietnam War and the Civil Rights Movement. Both of those entities challenged the military as it never had been before. And it would take years to recover, but it eventually did.

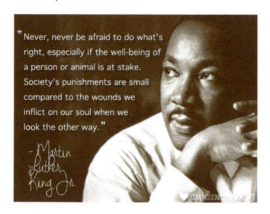

Back at March Air Force Base, the civil rights movement was playing out in full, as black power flew in the face of the "old guard." There were problems aplenty and the upper brass wanted solutions. I was one of about two dozen members of our squadron placed on a race relations board. Meeting once or twice a week, we were supposed to be working on a long-range plan to establish procedures on handling racially sensitive issues. In reality, we spent most of our time settling petty squabbles between two hostile groups. It was frustrating and soon became tedious.

Outside one end of our barracks, there were a bunch of tree stumps that hadn't been ground down or removed. The stumps actually provided a set of natural outdoor furniture, so black members of our barracks adopted this area as their hangout. They would be out there every day, late afternoon and into the night, partying, shooting dice, playing chess, executing the "dap" and of course doing "the dozens." The dap was a movement ritual that blacks made when greeting each other. Sometimes these greetings would take several minutes to execute. The dozens were an insult routine, that blacks would do with each other, to pass time. Both of these activities often made white people uncomfortable.

Some of the white members of our race relations board were invited to the Stump Gang festivities. I was one of those invited, and I visited the Stump Gang more than a few times, before I moved off base in the summer of 1971. And I thoroughly enjoyed my time with the Stumpers. There was always plenty to drink, great music, stimulating discussion and some damn fine barbecue.

I didn't always agree with the opinions of the more radicalized members of the group, especially the ones who advocated violence, but I empathized with many of their issues. The radical members were kept somewhat in check by the "leaders" of the Stump Gang, who earned their positions through experience, achievement and personality.

Three or four seasoned NCOs were those unofficial leaders of the Stump Gang, and of that group, Staff Sergeant H. Slaughter topped the list. A quiet, thoughtful individual, Slaughter also had charisma. He had done his time in Vietnam, and the other senior men in the gang looked up to him. Like me, Slaughter was just marking time until his discharge, and like me, the Air Force seemed to spend an inordinate amount of effort getting him to re-enlist. Apparently, they enjoyed the challenge. (They were unsuccessful in both cases.)

One of the rituals performed by the Stump Gang landed them outside the good graces of the upper brass. Everyone who drove or walked by the barracks was greeted with an extended middle finger. Though intended to be a harmless, inane gesture, it did not sit well with much of the "establishment." I was uncomfortable using it, and only participated in the ritual when I was absolutely sure no uppity ups were on the receiving end. (I antagonized the upper ranks enough without adding that to the pile.)

But a funny thing happened during those afternoons and evenings at the stumps. As the dozen or so whites interacted with the blacks in the Stump Gang, the two groups came to have a better understanding of each other. And through that better understanding, word got around, and after a time, procedures based upon mutual respect and understanding were written by the race relations board. There, while off duty and at leisure, solutions to racial disharmony availed themselves, and those solutions were passed along to the rest of the squadron, and to the base.

THE BIG SCREEN COMES TO PHU CAT

(Published in the MWSA Dispatches Winter 2018)

The play's the thing.

William Shakespeare

One of the nicer amenities provided by the U.S. military for American GIs in Vietnam was the opportunity to view feature films. (The word feature being highly subjective) Most medium and large U.S. military facilities had a movie theatre of one type or another. The real large bases in Danang and Saigon actually had indoor theaters, complete with air conditioning and concession stands. When I was in Danang for a short time I was able to catch an indoor movie while munching buttery popcorn in a reclining seat; at a nice cool 72 degrees. (Heaven on earth) I was never in Saigon, but I understand the theater at the air and army base there was every good as any large cinema back in the states.

The Phu Cat Airbase, though not as large as many other facilities in Vietnam, boasted a movie theater—albeit out door and somewhat Spartan. The small theater and stage was put up in 1968 specifically to host a USO show by Bob Hope and company. Standing on the edge of the base, the screen faced the western perimeter. While this solved a light pollution problem, it did provide somewhat of a security problem, as the men watching the late night entertainment now sat with their backs facing a very active (and dangerous) Vietnamese countryside. As a result of this security risk, all attendees were required to wear flak vests and helmets as they sat through the feature—keeping in mind that it was normally around ninety eight degrees Fahrenheit with the humidity being close to one hundred percent. And of course during the monsoon season the viewing audiences would be subjected to torrential rains. (But the show must go on.)

Being on the edge of the western perimeter provided a host of problems for the Phu Cat stage and theater.

The security problem manifested itself often, as a close inspection of the large screen revealed a surface pockmarked by bullet holes, both large and small caliber. The bullet and shrapnel holes, though patched up on a regular basis, were soon replaced by new ones. Rumor had it that one particular Vietcong sniper, who preferred westerns, would take pot shots at movies he didn't care for. I personally viewed several films at the theater and had to run for cover on two of those occasions. One was a short mortar attack not directed at the theater specifically, but a threat nonetheless. The other involved a VC (or other disgruntled film fan) sniper who shot at the movie screen during the film. Having been shot at before, I recognized the popping of air past my ears well before I heard the report of the weapon—and along with the others present, I scrambled for cover under the aluminum bench seats. Fortunately no one was hit that night.

It was no surprise to us that the VC or anyone else would take exception to the films, both from a quality or content stand point. Most of our supplies at Phu Cat came from the army facility at Qui Nhon, a coastal town about thirty miles away. From Qui Nhon our supplies and materials stopped at one or two other compounds in route before reaching Phu Cat. By the time the films arrived at Phu Cat, they were often in country for several months. The heat and humidity—not to mention wear and tear from repeated use—wore them down considerably.

Our films usually broke several times during the performance much to the chagrin of the film projector who was known to one and all as "Lester." (What else?) Outside of the local VC, who often ruined our sleep with their shenanigans, our film projector "Lester" was the most despised man at Phu Cat. We often had the same movie for weeks, and only out of insane boredom could I drag myself to go see some of them. The movies were mostly old westerns from the thirties, forties and fifties, and if any of them got close to seeing an Academy

Award it would have been only through geography perhaps. How many people remember "Johnny Mac Brown?" Yep…not exactly top-flight entertainment.

USO shows drew GIs from far and wide

When the film broke, as aforementioned, the viewing crowd went after Lester like an angry lynch mob. They showered him with obscenities, and threw debris at his little projection booth in the middle of the viewing stands. On several occasions he was dragged out of the booth and beaten, prompting the Apes (Air Police) to be summoned to quell the disturbance. I felt sorry for the guy—kind of like one does for Barney Fife on the Andy Griffith show. You gleefully know a disaster will occur that Barney is responsible for, yet you're glad when Andy takes pity and bails him out. Unfortunately Andy wasn't anywhere near Phu Cat and old Lester took more abuse than a telemarketer at supper time. I often wondered how poor old Lester got stuck with that duty. Between VC snipers and the surly audience, Marines at Khe Sanh took less abuse that Lester.

The newly installed electrical grid on base provided plenty of power for the theatre and any accessories required. A stage was built in front of the screen and in addition to the Bob Hope show in '68, many other USO shows were held there as well. The USO contracted with many Asian entertainment groups to perform for American GIs in Vietnam. Korean, Filipino and Thai bands performed often and "Plowed Maly" along with many other pop favorites would be belted out, albeit with a unique Asian dialect.

After an internal investigation by the U.S. military during that time, it was revealed that a group of senior NCOs responsible for the USO shows in Vietnam were skimming off the top. (Reference my book *The Kansas NCO*) This was no surprise to anyone, as the same performers visited Phu Cat over and over again—no matter how bad they were.

The quality of the musical performances was often determined by the amount of alcohol the audience had consumed—despite it having been barred from these events. However the bands knew what the American GIs really came for and they gave it to them. Each band contained several young girls who, scantily clad, would gyrate to the music in the steaming Vietnamese heat. The young, robust GIs, months away from home, would yell, scream and dance along with the nubile young women, while pressing as close to the stage as they could. Security police kept a close watch on these performances as GIs would often encroach upon the stage while attempting to grope the dancers. Performances were stopped on many occasions as hordes of lustful men would breach the stage all at one time. When this happened the entertainers would flee in terror as the beleaguered and badly outnumbered security police would futilely attempt to stop the surge of alcohol-fueled, hormonal-crazed GIs.

Despite the questionable quality, you couldn't keep GIs away from these shows with a gun. (Which was often tried, as previously noted.) Entertainment was at a premium and any chance to get away from the glum reality of the war was taken. Troops who came in out of the field took advantage of the theater as much as they could. Some just came to grab a place to sleep. If they caught any part of the show, so be it, but they enjoyed their short respite from life in the bush. Local villagers would often sit outside the wire and watch the entertainment as well. Come darkness, however, they would melt away into the night—as the territory was now occupied by Vietcong and trigger happy American perimeter guards.

And despite any problems regarding the movies and USO shows, any GI who served in Vietnam has fond memories of those movies and shows, and probably photos as well. Bob Hope, Ann Margaret, Chris Noel, James Brown, Sammy Davis Jr, Martha Raye, Raquel Welch and many other performers took time out of their lives and schedules to visit and entertain us in Vietnam. It wasn't easy for them either. They had to deal with the heat, the monsoons, the bugs and the VC just as we did. And thanks also to the many Asian performers who provided us with entertainment…of all kinds.

But we can still look back and chuckle at the various adventures and misadventures surrounding our outdoor theater at Phu Cat. And Lester…if you're still out there somewhere…thanks for taking all that abuse and showing us those great films back in the day!

Johnny's Saloon

(Published in MWSA Dispatches, Winter 2021 edition)

Places of intrigue drew us in, like bees to honey.

Joe

From December of 1968 to December of 1969 I was stationed at Grand Forks Air Force Base in North Dakota. The sprawling airbase was about fifteen miles from the town of Grand Forks and was primarily a SAC (Strategic Air Command) base, containing a full complement of B-52 Bombers. Grand Forks was also home to the 18th Fighter Interceptor Squadron, an ADC (Air Defense Command) unit, consisting of Voodoo F-101 Fighter Interceptors. I was a member of the F-101 Fighter squadron.

I'm a Blue Fox for life

The desolate area was frozen and windswept for much of the year, and holds the honor of being the second coldest spot in the continental United States, just behind its frosty neighbor to the north, International Falls, Minnesota.

For bachelor airmen of low rank, options for entertainment were limited. There was an Airmen's Club open two days a week, a base theater, and a gym. Most of us, however, spent much of our off-duty time in our barracks. That's where the real partying went on. If we were lucky, we might snag a ride to the town of Grand Forks from one of the more senior members of our squadron. Occasionally we would walk to town, covering the fifteen-mile trek twice in one day, unless we found somewhere to stay over till the next day. In the bitter winter months, walking to town was not an option.

Part 1: War and Military Stories

Right along side every major U.S. military installation there is usually a small town consisting of a cluster of businesses that cater to those on base. Whatever product or service you couldn't manage to find on base, the small group of entrepreneurs, within walking distance of the main gate, unencumbered by military convention, rules or regulations would provide you with almost anything you should so desire. The name of the town outside of Grand Forks Air Force Base was Emerado.

In 1968, Emerado, North Dakota, consisted of a handful of hard scrabble dwellings, one tavern called Johnny's Saloon, and one diner known as Lou's Café. There was also a small fair ground where two or three times a year traveling carnivals would set-up shop providing cotton candy, various carny rides for the Air Force dependent children, and a host of slight-of-hand gamesters who fleeced naive airmen out of whatever cash they carried with them. Often these carnivals left in a hurry when word got out of major scamming activities.

Johnny's Saloon in Emerado, North Dakota is still in business!

Like many of my peers at the airbase, I was drawn to the earthy charms of the small community of Emerado. Johnny's Saloon was a real old west type honky tonk. It offered tap and bottle beer, several types of hard liquor, a juke box featuring country & western and rock, and usually a couple of dust ups every night. The air police from base would, on occasion, have to come to Johnny's when major brawls involving base airmen broke out. Otherwise the occasional state trooper would be called in to dispense justice and restore order. Once order was restored, the trooper would usually stay for a beverage or two.

Lou's Café, owned by a large reticent woman (named Lou), served hamburgers, hot dogs and a very thin, spicy no frills chili. The joke was if you couldn't finish your chili at Lou's, you could always take it with you and lube the axles on your vehicle with it. If any customer asked Lou for her chili recipe, she merely scowled and said "grease." She had a captive customer base and needn't perform any airs or jump through hoops to bring them in. Airmen from the base in various stages of sobriety filtered in and out of Lou's all night long, seven days a week.

Whether we went to Lou's or not, we'd usually finish off our nights at Johnny's Saloon. The back deck of Johnny's faced the north and on many winter evenings the Aurora Borealis provided a beautiful light show for all those in attendance. I have fond memories of sitting on a picnic table at Johnny's Saloon, drinking beer and watching the fascinating gyrations of the northern lights.

The Northern Lights were mesmerizing

I left North Dakota in December of 1969 with orders to Vietnam. In Vietnam, I witnessed a light show almost every night as well, though one of a much different nature.

NOAH, HOOCH DOG AND STAR OF THE SILVER SCREEN?

Published in MWSA Dispatches Spring 2020 edition.

It seems I had been drawn into another lost cause.

Joe

NOAH, FUTURE STAR OF THE SILVER SCREEN?

Our tick ridden, flea bitten friend Noah.

As many know, most of the characters in my books are based on real people. However, one character in my book, Noah, probably has more true to life attributes than most of the others included in my writing. Noah, our hooch* dog at Phu Cat airbase in Vietnam, was quite a character and his mannerisms and behavior are reflected in my book *The Kansas NCO*, and also in the recent screenplay, written by Charrisa Gracyk. So, Noah, our flea-bitten, tick-ridden, C-rat mooching hooch dog may someday be immortalized on the silver screen. How in the heck did that happen?

Tim's dog

Noah would never be mistaken for Lassie.

Tim, one of my good friends in Vietnam, was the one who first "adopted" Noah. Noah, like most dogs in the Nam, ran in a pack with other feral dogs. I don't exactly know how Noah got separated from the pack and became the responsibility of Tim, but one day, much to the chagrin to the rest of us who had to deal with him, there came Tim, with Noah on his heels.

Not enthralled with the little bugger, I was only one of many who was unwelcoming to Noah. He was about as mangy of a mutt as I had ever seen. As he trotted across the hooch, ticks fell off him like water off a duck's back. As a bonus, he smelled just like the nearby vermin filled swamp, which fairly steamed in the oppressive Vietnamese heat.

While off duty, Tim would spend hours picking ticks and fleas off of Noah's scroungy little carcass. A four-legged Romeo, Noah was constantly pestering females in his and other packs as well, earning him a good drubbing at least once a day. (Noah even tried to cozy up with the female German Shepherds from the Canine Corps.) The ever-loyal Tim provided first aid to all of Noah's bites and scratches. I guess we should have felt fortunate that Tim didn't adopt one of the local monkeys, as some others had done. Those monkeys, though cute, were nastier than a badger in a bee hive and would bite the heck out of anything within reach. (Our little Noah, on occasion, would also incur their wrath.)

A Dog's Life During the War

The war was no kinder to animals than it was to humans. The feral dogs were often caught up in various offensive activities at hand, with many being killed as collateral damage in any number of engagements. Battles with other packs, starvation and disease also took their toll, as did providing the local villagers with an additional source of protein. It wasn't much of a life for the canine critters.

The feral dogs ran around in packs for survival purposes. Of course, many packs consisted of dogs related to each other. I'm not sure how Noah got separated from his pack, but one of the packs in the area of our hooch was certainly his. Noah wasn't kept on a chain or anything, he was free to run around at will and mostly did when we weren't around. I'm sure he hung with his old pack during those times.

One day, after a mortar attack on our base, Noah didn't turn up for a while. Worried, we later found him near the body of another dog which was laying in the road dead, killed by one of the incoming mortars. Noah lay quiet with his head on the other dog's body. From the looks of the other dog, we were pretty sure it must have been Noah's mother. Noah moped around for a day or two, but was soon back to his mischievous self.

The Worm Turns for Noah.

After nine months of "fun" in Vietnam, I took my R & R. Eight great days in Hong Kong. I left with some trepidation, however, as Noah would now have to fend for himself. (Tim had went home and left Noah in my care). I wasn't too worried about him finding enough food, he was a class A scrounger and also a class A beggar. I was concerned, however, about his ability to defend himself, as the many detractors he had would have happily dispatched him, given the chance. And as previously mentioned, dogs were on the menu of the local Vietnamese—and my good friends, the Korean ROK soldiers who protected our western perimeter, also had a fondness for canine cuisine. After I returned from R & R and the dust settled, I pondered Noah's fate.

Wonder if that damn mutt's still around.

My question was soon answered as much to my surprise, I found Noah in the company of "the brothers" who were petting him fondly and serving up treats. You could have knocked me over with a feather, as they say, as previously Noah had received much abuse from many of the black members of our unit. They had little patience for him, and often gave poor old Tim a ration of manure regarding the flea-bitten pest he had brought into their midst. This turn of a affairs was indeed startling, however the reason behind Noah's sudden change of status was even more startling.

No match for Noah!

As the story goes, one day while I was on my R&R, Noah surprised and attacked a cobra that had slithered into our barracks. The large snakes would often enter our dwellings, as the dwellings were inhabited by large rats who came in for shelter and left-over food. Though a danger to us as well, the cobras were primarily after the rats, which was one of their primary food sources.

Those who witnessed the incident claimed Noah and the snake fought for almost fifteen minutes before Noah subdued the reptile by biting it behind the head and shaking it mightily. After the battle, Noah, himself bitten several times, laid down for the rest of the day. Feared dead, no one thought to get him any medical attention. But plucky Noah, after only one day, was up and around and back to his old self.

NOAH SAYS GOODBYE

After the cobra incident, I was off the hook regarding Noah's care. That worked out well, since most of my last couple of months in Vietnam were spent in a small Korean army (the ROKs) bunker on our western perimeter. And although I was made comfortable among those stalwart warriors, like the Vietnamese, the Koreans would have happily added Noah to the dinner menu.

Some good byes were harder than others.

During my last couple of days in Vietnam, I visited the local orphanage one more time, spent time with our old mama san and her family and visited the kids who hung around the main gate selling "stuff." (They always thought I was a mark.) I said goodbye one more time to all of my friends—American, Vietnamese and Korean.

An Air Force pick-up truck took me and my gear to the flight line, where I would leave Phu Cat on a C-130 to Cam Ranh Bay. About two days later I'd get on a Flying Tigers DC-8 Freedom bird for that long-awaited trip back home.

While still at Phu Cat, I was surprised when Noah showed up at the hooch and ran behind my pick-up truck all the way to the flight line. Once out processed, I sat on the flight line with the little rascal, until it was time to board. I gave him one last bit of petting and told him to watch over mama san and baby san for me. He gave me one last mischievous look, turned around and trotted away.

*Hooch: any dwelling or living quarters

THE FALL OF SAIGON

Published in the Kenosha News, 4/30/2020

Indeed, history is nothing more than a tableau of crimes and misfortunes.

Voltaire

A SAD DAY IN HISTORY

April 30, 2020 marks the 45th anniversary of the Fall of Saigon. An ignoble day in which the communist North Vietnamese completed their take over of South Vietnam.

As a Vietnam War veteran, I well remember that day. After the completion of my military service in 1972, following a brief visit home, I relocated to Southern California where I would spend two years kicking around, scratching for employment. With a weak economy and no higher-level skills, I finally moved back to Wisconsin and stayed with the folks until I was able to land a decent paying job.

I ended up working with a company in northern Illinois, who's owner, a very decent man, went out of his way to hire Vietnam Veterans. Not a practice enthusiastically followed during that time.

I started out working in the factory, in final assembly. In our immediate area, almost half of us were Vietnam War veterans—Army, Navy, Marines and Air Force, we were all there. We seldom talked about the war. It was not a popular topic during that time, not even with each other. But we did kid one another about our particular branches of the service. Mostly good natured, but it could heat up at times.

The fall of Saigon was not a surprise to us…or anyone else for that matter, but when it finally happened it created a somberness, all across our nation, and certainly in our little world on that factory floor.

We were the lucky ones. The South Vietnamese, who we were fighting for, were brutally punished by their North Vietnamese conquerors. Even the Vietcong, allies of the North Vietnamese, were pushed off to one side and trodden under. North Vietnam, with the charismatic Ho Chi Minh having passed on, carried out the aftermath of the war as a cold, vengeful master.

YEARS IN THE MAKING

Colonial France dominated Vietnam for many years.

The origins of the "American War" in Vietnam can be traced back to the Truman administration. However, the root cause of the war was French colonialism and our eventual support of it.

Truman got roped into helping the French when communism was taking over many nations in post-World War II Europe. He agreed to help France in Vietnam, if France would crack down on the communist party in France, which they did.

Eisenhower maintained Truman's policy in Southeast Asia and little by little, America unleashed the dogs of war. By 1965, after the Gulf of Tonkin fiasco played out, the U.S. was in hook, line and sinker.

From Truman to Nixon, every U.S. president maintained the war.

The war lumbered along, with increasing carnage on both sides of the conflict. The U.S., a military powerhouse, found the North Vietnamese and the Vietcong to be a tenacious foe. Bank rolled by Red China and the Soviet Union, the communist regime proved once again that the price of victory surpassed the cost of human sacrifice, in their world.

Soon other nations became embroiled in the conflict as Lyndon Johnson's "All Nations" policy dragged South Korea, the Philippines, Thailand and Australia into the quagmire.

Regime after regime in South Vietnam collapsed, as corruption, military defeat and political, religious and ethnic turmoil played out. In the meantime, Americans at home who were scratching their heads regarding the logic of the war became increasingly disenchanted.

After the massive North Vietnamese TET offensive in early 1968, support of the war in the United states began to unravel. Although a huge military defeat for the communists, Americans felt, not without reason, that they were misled as to the progress of the war.

By 1970, when I served in Vietnam, Richard Nixon had assumed the presidency and, although he claimed a policy of "Peace with Honor," both he and his architect of the war, Henry Kissinger, knew the war was already hopeless. The American people had had enough.

Without getting into the ensuing politics of the war, suffice to say that the eventual American withdrawal led to the collapse of South Vietnam. On April 30th, 1975 Saigon (Now Ho Chi Minh City) fell to the North Vietnamese army.

The Aftermath

The flag of communist Vietnam

As previously noted, the vengeful North punished their South Vietnamese brethren viciously, for many years to come. Re-education camps, executions, beatings, torture, and forfeiture of rights were all visited upon the hapless citizens of South Vietnam.

Those who could, fled. Between 1975 and 1995 close to two million Vietnamese fled the vindictive communist regime. Many of those who fled perished in the process, victims of murder, drowning, starvation and disease. Those who did make it found themselves scattered all over the globe, with many ending up in Australia, Europe and the U.S.

The Vietnamese who have made the United States their home are model citizens, contributing much to the melting pot, that we are. A hardworking people who appreciate the benefits of education, culture and service, our gain is Communist Vietnam's loss.

As time has gone on, the Communist regime has become more and more capitalistic. The underlying work ethic of the Vietnamese cannot be repressed by the false ideology of a failed system—and for all intents and purposes, Vietnam is migrating into the enlightened camp, albeit with much work yet to be done.

Dedication

This article is dedicated to the hundreds of thousands of Vietnamese who had the courage to leave their homeland for the price of freedom. And also to those millions, from all nations, who perished during the war and it's aftermath.

In Closing

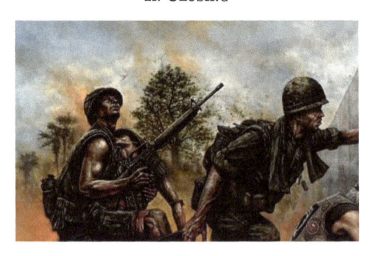

I didn't want a monument,

Not even one as sober as that vast black wall of broken lives.

I didn't want a postage stamp,

I didn't want a road beside the Delaware river proclaiming Vietnam Veterans Memorial Highway.

What I wanted was a simple recognition of the limits of our power as a nation to inflict our will upon others.

What I wanted was an understanding that the world is neither black and white, nor ours.

What I wanted was an end to monuments.

Author, unknown

THE ORPHANS

> We were castoffs and slaves, orphans and unwanteds and used-to-be princesses... and we were mighty.
>
> Lesley Livingston, "The Valiant"

One of the many unfortunate by-products of war are orphans. The orphanages near our base at Phu Cat, Vietnam were visited by the base chaplains who brought sustenance in the way of food, clothing, and other goods, as well as spiritual support. GI volunteers often accompanied them, bringing their own small supply of treats for the children. I went along on several of these visits.

The experience was both enlightening and saddening. On one occasion I brought a tin of hard Christmas candies my mother had sent. The clamoring children literally ripped the buttons off of my shirt as I tried handing them out.

The saddest part of these visits was watching the children vie for the attention of the American GIs, hoping against hope that they might be adopted and delivered from the hell that was their lives. The ones with missing limbs and other war scars, stood humbly back as the "less damaged" children jockeyed for position. Those memories are forever etched in my mind.

Section 2

Outdoor Recreation and Leisure

Joe has had many outdoor adventures over the years. Some good...some not so good. But many were interesting for sure, and in this section we take a look at some of them.

Perch Fishing in Old Kenosha

Published in Our Wisconsin Magazine, Aug/Sep 2017

Every fishing trip is a new adventure, a new story, a new memory.

Joe

Growing up in Kenosha, Wisconsin, along the shores of Lake Michigan provided many adventures in swimming and fishing for those of us who lived there. For any kid raised back in the day, Lake Michigan perch fishing was always a favorite activity, both spring and summer.

My Dad after rolling his jeep in Europe during WWII. His favorite activity was perch fishing.

Before salmon and trout fishing took hold, lake perch were the top catch of the lake. Many of us would scramble down to its cold shores early in the morning in hopes of catching a batch of the tasty little critters. I, like many of my peers at that time, had a morning paper route from Henoch News Agency, so I had to finish delivering the papers before doing anything else. But once done, the side baskets of my bike which had just been full of newspapers now contained my fishing gear—and along with my brother and/or friends, off we went.

Our dads had introduced us to perch fishing at an early age and many of them would head down on weekends, or mornings when they didn't have to work. When Dad went along we rode in the car in style! First thing we did was hit the bait shop to pick up a couple dozen "shiners." The little minnows were usually all that was needed to catch a nice fat perch. But the real die hard perchers preferred crayfish tails, commonly referred to as crab tails, or just crawdads.

Crabs as they were called could be caught at night at the Lincoln Lagoon or Pikes Creek, among other places. All one needed was a flashlight and a willingness to get wet feet. This activity itself could turn into an adventure. The critters would be hiding under submerged rocks and logs in shallow water. Just flip the rock over and grab the wily crayfish before it scooted away. Once in a while a crayfish would be found inside an old can it crawled in and couldn't get out of as a result of its own growth. Meat from the crab tails would often catch the biggest perch, and the guys having crab meat for bait were high on the pecking order of fishermen at the lakefront.

Bamboo poles were king.

A routine stop at the bait shop landed me in hot water with my dad for a whole summer one year. Back in those days, most everyone fished with bamboo cane poles. Nothing fancy, some had one extension, some two, and some even three—in order to get them out over the water farther. The line was wrapped around the end section of the pole for travel and storage. Some fisherman had little wooden boards which they sat on that had holders for two cane poles. Those guys were taken seriously. My dad had two, three section cane poles and the "serious" seat with the holders. Some of the old timers had bait casting reels sitting at home—and a few of the young "whippersnappers" had some of the new spin cast reels that Zebco pushed out faster than Ford dealers pumped out Falcons. However, serious perchers disdained the "fancy" gear, brushing it off with a frown, "You don't need dat!"

On one particular fishing excursion, it was my job to load the car with the cane poles and tackle. I carelessly slipped the poles through the open back window paying no heed to where they landed. A section of the poles remained sticking out the window, but of course I was clueless to the impending disaster. Sure enough, when we pulled in front of the bait shop, the pole sticking out the farthest hit a small road sign next to the curb, and with a loud crack it snapped like a twig run over by a garbage truck.

The sharp report of fracturing bamboo got everyone's attention including my dad who, immediately assessing the damage was now looking at me red with rage. (My dad had that look pretty much nailed.) I knew I was in trouble. It was, of course, his favorite pole. Luckily I was out of his reach in the backseat behind him, as he flailed away with his right hand. Back then parents were still allowed, even encouraged, to give a kid a good beating when called for. My dad was a strong advocate of this policy.

After he settled down, I made a pathetic attempt to see if the splintered bamboo pole would possibly fit back together…no deal on that one. Now, as I was obligated to replace it, much of my paper route money for the next couple of weeks went to that cause, forcing me to mooch money for bait and other sundries off of my brother and friends, who learned to avoid me like the plague. And every trip after that incident, my dad inspected the packing of the poles as if they were nuclear tipped missiles being placed in launch silos.

The location we fished with Dad was set in stone. Although perch could be caught all up and down the Kenosha shoreline, most of them were caught in the main boat harbor downtown. Two piers, built many years ago, extend out several hundred feet into the lake to compose the large boat harbor. These are referred to as the north pier and the south pier. This is important, because in the perch fishing culture of Kenosha, you were either a north pier guy or a south pier guy. If a person from either one was to fish at the opposite pier, they would come under derision from their peers. This was serious stuff. North pier guys and south pier guys didn't mix. End of story.

The Kenosha Harbor as it looks today. Photo by Cindi Fredericksen.

By the sixties, both piers were in considerable disrepair and required caution when walking on them. The middle sections were hollow and full of rip rap.

These were favorite playgrounds and hiding places for young kids (and late night drunken indigents) who accompanied their elders for a couple hours of fishing. Each one had a cat walk that was occasionally traveled on, once again by playing youngsters or testosterone filled teens at night.

The south pier had only one side facing water so the fishermen there were at a slight disadvantage. The north pier was surrounded by water on both sides, and although the side facing the harbor usually produced more fish, both sides would on occasion—and on slow days—be in use as fishermen moved from one side to the other in search of a bite. But in spite of the north pier advantage you couldn't get a south pier guy over there on a bet. My dad, being an old north pier guy, was quite put out when one of his brothers defected to the south pier one year. You'd have thought he committed a crime against the family. My dad would talk to him after that, but the conversations were limited.

The piers being adjacent, fishermen on the south wall of the north pier and fisherman on the south pier facing north were well within eye and ear shot of each other. Occasionally they tossed taunts and derisive comments at their competitors. When the fish came in, each side anxiously eyed the other, hoping they wouldn't be out-fished by their cross-pier rivals.

As the perch entered the harbor in large schools, the fishermen toward the outer ends of the piers started catching fish first. The guys farther down the pier could see many of the cane poles coming up one right after another with a "fish on." This would be a busy time with much yelling and jabbering going on. The guys with two poles, and more than one hook on would sometimes get two "double headers" on at once.

After a time, the school of fish—having made it past the gauntlet of fishermen to forage around the interior of the harbor—went back out into the lake. The simultaneous raising of cane polls began again, only this time starting at the opposite end of the piers. The fishing usually tapered off by mid-morning and those who had filled their buckets swaggered off the pier with their prize and their gear. Those remaining looked on enviously—and knowing they had some catching up to do—and hunkered down. Anything less than a third of a bucket of perch and, well…"Might as well as stayed home!"

By one or one thirty, even the most diehard fishermen knew it was time to throw in the towel. By now the swimmers were out on the pier running around, disrupting the tactics of our skilled anglers. Fishermen could only put up with so much nonsense. Once the screaming kids took over, the remaining perchers usually vacated in short order.

Once home the prized catch was shown off to anyone within eye or ear shot. The fish were taken out back to the picnic table along with the scaler, a knife, and some old newspaper. Few people filleted the perch back then. If you didn't like picking through bones, well maybe you were a "buncha old ladies."

After the catch was cleaned, the guts were usually dug into the family garden and the rest of the debris was wrapped in newspaper and discarded in the garbage can to ferment in the summer sun. The old newspapers kept the odor at bay for about 3 hours whereupon they reached a fine ambiance which had the effect of catnip on all the local felines. Most nights they could be heard squabbling with each other in the middle of the night. Mornings involved a clean-up operation of the previous night's feast.

Although some people had chest freezers at the time, the perch were often kept in the "ice box" till Friday night for the family fish fry. Mothers battered the perch and fried them in hot oil in the cast iron frying pan. They served French fries, homemade coleslaw, and rye bread along with the perch. Dad might have a beer or two and the kids had a soda if they were lucky—milk if not—to wash the tasty feast down. Dads all over town grunted, "Dats great."

Soon after, a retreat to the living room just in time for Gunsmoke, and another fine Friday night was had, along the shores of Lake Michigan.

Ma & Pa Kettle

I had rather be on my farm than be emperor of the world.

George Washington

Whenever autumn arrives, my thoughts turn to pheasant hunting—one of my favorite activities throughout the years. My best friend Jim and I hunted and fished together until he passed away unexpectedly some time back. Over all that time, we had many fine adventures in the woods and on the water.

We started hunting in the "Teapot Woods" in Kenosha, Wisconsin, when we were just sprouts in grade school. The Teapot was within easy riding distance on our bicycles—and we could walk there as well. It was adjacent to Vern Irons farm—and when wild game enticed us to cross over onto Vern's property, we harbored no ill will when he chased us out with his shotgun. It was a tradition.

My son Billy after one of our pheasant hunts.

As time passed, we fished all over Wisconsin including Lake Michigan for perch and smelt, the Mississippi River for Walleye and catfish…and all points in between. As we grew older, we expanded our hunting and fishing territory to include much of the Midwest. We graced Northern Ontario in Canada with our presence as well.

Now Jim and I were not what you would refer to as the consummate sportsmen. We didn't much care if our tackle box was a wreck. Untangling lures might be considered a sport in some places, you never know. And if our shotgun had a bent stock, why we just bent along with it while shooting. We would never win any trap shooting patches—or fly-tying trophies for that matter. We didn't always get up at the crack of dawn, although we often went to bed around that time. And we didn't always brush after each meal or clean our guns after each use…but I doubt few people had a better time at it than we did.

Jim's parents had a small cottage in central Wisconsin and we had many fine days fishing and hunting up there over the years. When we were of age to drive and had the run of the place, all bets were off! Any number of adventures and "miss-adventures" took place. One of our favorite haunts was a nearby nightclub for young people. Jim was convinced that the musk sold to attract bucks in the fall, would also attract young girls at the club. However the scent apparently had the opposite effect on them—sometimes creating an awkward scene requiring a hasty retreat. No matter, we danced to our own drummer and enjoyed the hell out of ourselves!

Jim, Mel, Don and myself on a Canadian fishing trip many years ago.

Of all the hunting trips we had, hunting pheasants and rabbits on the farm owned by Jim's aunt and uncle was always our favorite—hands down. The farm was located about thirty miles outside of Rockford, Illinois along the Pecatonica River. For a long time, we visited the farm several times a year during the fall and winter, chasing cottontails and those wily ring neck pheasants.

Ma & Pa Kettle

Jim's Aunt and Uncle were a hoot. His aunt, the typical bustling farm woman, directed the pace of operations for her rather laid back husband. They were very much like Ma and Pa Kettle of the old film series starring Marjorie Main and Percy Kilbride…and that's how we always referred to them.

The farm consisted of about four hundred acres of corn and soybeans, along with a dozen or so dairy cattle, several beef cattle plus numerous chickens and ducks. We usually spent two or three days there during our visit, helping out with farm chores in exchange for room, board and hunting privileges.

Our rooms were on the second floor of Ma and Pa's ancient farm house. The heat source up there was a grated hole in the ceiling which allowed warm air from the first floor to migrate to the second floor. On cold winter nights, you could see your breath up there and we often slept wearing every article of clothing we had with us.

Mornings consisted of a large farm breakfast including fresh chicken or duck eggs, thick bacon and homemade biscuits. As we arrived downstairs for breakfast, Pa would be coming in from the barn or field, having already been up a couple of hours tending to farm chores. After breakfast, we hung around in the hot kitchen still trying to warm up a bit. Then we gathered our gear and headed out for the first hunt of the day.

We always started out in the barn. Wild pigeons roosted in the upper loft, feeding on Pa's grain and making a mess. Pa encouraged us to shoot as many of them as we could. Our strategy here was to have one guy inside the barn who would raise hell, causing the pigeons to flush out of the very upper barn window. The second guy shot at the birds as they flew out. Now that may sound easy, but those pigeons came out of there like they were shot out of a cannon, and whenever we hit any it was mostly pure luck.

One day Jim and I hatched a plan to outsmart the pigeons. We both raised Caine inside the barn and tried to shoot them BEFORE they flew out. In our "exuberance" we managed to hit the roof several times aerating it for extra ventilation and future rain showers. Pa Kettle, being Pa Kettle, didn't raise his voice or lose his temper. He just made us go up on the barn roof with him for the necessary repairs. Pa had a ladder that would make a fireman green with envy, easily reaching the edge of the barn roof. Now up there, Jim and I clung to the ladder in terror, hanging on like the plane was going down. Our obvious discomfort amused Pa who chuckled happily while he patched up the roof.

Needless to say we never implemented that shooting strategy again.

After we addressed the pigeon problem, we tackled another source of irritation for Pa. The corn cribs and grain silos near the barn were plagued by rabbits who would feed all night on Pa's grain and then rest nearby during the day. Keeping in mind our morning of terror on the barn roof, we loaded our shotguns with number 8 shot to avoid any damage to the silos and cribs. After popping a few bunnies, we dropped them off with Ma who let out a cackle and threw them into her porch storage bin. Later in the day, she cleaned them—and at some point in the future, they appeared on the menu.

Having put the pigeons and rabbits on notice, we now got down to the business of what we came for—pheasant hunting. Pa's farm and the adjacent area was home to a nice population of wild ring necks who were fat, colorful and cagey. Normally hunting pheasants without a dog is an effort in futility, however with so many birds in and around the farm, we were always able to flush plenty of them ourselves. We walked to the end of the farm and worked a hedgerow next to a corn or soybean field. The birds ran along ahead. However, one of us positioned himself at the end of the hedgerow, while the other pushed the birds along. Both of us usually got plenty of shooting when the surprised birds flushed at the end of said hedgerow. We worked each hedgerow on the farm throughout the day. During the years we hunted Ma and Pa Kettle's farm, private property in Illinois had no wild game limit so we could take as many as we wanted.

Pheasants on the wing.

Usually in early afternoon we broke for lunch and a short nap. Ma would always have a great spread for us, and knowing that she put on that great feast, Pa made sure he came in from his chores at the same time and joined us.

After a short siesta, we often visited Jim's cousin who lived nearby with his young family. His cousin worked for American Breeders Society and artificially inseminated cattle for local farmers. This occupation fascinated Jim and me and we accompanied him on his rounds. As he worked, he told us plenty of jokes relating to his occupation—including a number of humorous stories about trysts with cows that had gone bad. He showed us how he cautiously approached the "promising" Heifer in waiting, and how he stood with his legs slightly bent so when the inevitable kicks came, his legs wouldn't get broken. He offered to let both of us have a crack at the task, however with discretion being the better part of valor, we turned him down. The thought of possible rejection by a young bovine in heat left us hesitant to tackle the job. Or worse yet, the fear of an over-zealous love-struck, six-hundred-pound cow mauling us in a barn was more than our pride (and bodies) could probably stand.

Jim's cousin was also a trapper and after his cattle-breeding chores were done, we accompanied him as he worked his trap-line along the Pecatonica River. Jim and I proved to be no better at trapping than we were at breeding love-sick bovines, but we enjoyed watching his cousin deftly handle that pursuit as well.

One thing we learned regarding farmers, they hold to a schedule. Having learned that early on, we made sure we were back on the farm in time for Ma Kettle's supper, which was even better than her fantastic lunches. After supper, Jim and I headed to an area where we knew the pheasants came in to roost for the night. We usually got plenty of shooting in, hunting until dusk.

At the end of each visit, we coaxed Ma and Pa into letting us take them out to the local supper club. The two of us were poor farmhands, and worse carpenters. Outside of leaving Ma and Pa with some rabbits and pheasants, we had no other way to repay them for their hospitality. Pa Kettle was all for it and enjoyed an evening out immensely, but the ever practical Ma Kettle fussed about it like she was going for a tooth extraction. "Can't see spending good money on a little dinner that we can make at home," she'd mutter. We usually brought some wine with us and if we got her to drink a few glasses before supper, we could soften her up for the outing. Once out she fretted about her appearance and the cost we would incur, but enjoyed herself in spite of her own objections.

The next morning, after another great breakfast, they handed us a box of homemade preserves and sent us on our way, concluding another fine visit with Ma and Pa Kettle!

Man Overboard!

Smell the sea and feel the sky, let your soul and spirits fly!

Van Morrison

My wife Ann and I have been on two cruises. Our first cruise, shortly after we married, was on a ship called the *Tropicale* of the Carnival Cruise line. The eight day cruise departed out of Los Angeles, California, and sailed for two days down to Puerto Vallarta, Mexico, where we then stayed for two more days. We took an excursion tour of Puerto Vallarta with a resident guide who took us directly to one of his relatives' taverns, and then to another relative's tourist shop. He then left us at a highly touted restaurant on the far outskirts of town. Problem was before departing, he failed to mention it had been closed for several months. Ann and I elected to hike back to the cruise ship—not something I'd recommend in this day and age. Upon leaving Puerto Vallarta, we cruised to Mazatlán for a one day stay, then Cabo San Lucas for a day, and after that we headed back to the home port of LA. Other than a few minor incidents such as our less than reputable tour guide in Puerto Vallarta, we encountered no problems and enjoyed the trip very much. We also got to visit with our friend George Dooley and his son Steven at port in LA before we made way. After the trip we both agreed that we'd definitely go on another cruise, given the chance.

About ten years later, we got to take that second cruise. This was a five day cruise to the Bahamas on a ship called the *Nordic Empress* of the Royal Carib-

Joe and Ann

The Tropicale

bean cruise line. We boarded in Miami, Florida and headed for the Bahamas where we anchored off a small island that the cruise line owned. We enjoyed the beautiful water and marine life while snorkeling around the island until Ann got stung on the knee by fire coral. I pretended I knew what to do by rubbing aspirin powder on her knee every half hour or so. It actually helped quite a bit so she was quite impressed. Up until that point, I had only used my medical skills one other time, treating a burn victim at a local night club. The results of that incident insured me of a short medical career.

Nordic Empress

After the *Nordic Empress* left the small island where we had been snorkeling, we went to Nassau where we spent a day and a half in port there. As Ann was still ailing with her knee, I struck out alone. I rented a small moped to tour the island. Once out on the road, the throttle stuck wide open and I had a difficult time controlling the bike. It was a pretty wild ride. I circled the island many times. I was forced into some real defensive driving in heavy traffic, and had a couple close calls. After I complained to the vendor about the shoddy bike he had rented me, he tried to blow it off, but I persisted until he finally refunded my money.

Upon leaving Nassau, our ship headed back for the home port of Miami. In the afternoon an unusual announcement came over the loudspeaker. Apparently a passenger on one of the ships ahead of us had fallen overboard. We were alerted in the unlikely event that we might see someone bobbing around in the water. We learned that many cruise ships traveled the same shipping lanes one after another and we would be sailing through water some ships ahead of us had already passed through, so it wasn't totally beyond the realm that the person might be spotted.

Late that evening after enjoying some on board entertainment, Ann and I were returning to our cabin when we encountered a chaotic scene on the first deck. A gathering of passengers (many in an inebriated state) and crew members were clamoring around the deck rail, throwing ropes at something in the water. Low and behold, in the dark murky water, a life buoy with dim flashing lights could be seen. With eyes focused you could just about make out the head and shoulders of a person in the buoy.

As the crowd thickened, the rescue operation was in peril, with more drunken passengers yelling and shouting what should or shouldn't be done. Finally a senior crew member appeared and took charge. He ordered the passengers back and directed the crew to one of the lifeboats closest to the bobbing life buoy in the water. The buoy and its occupant were rapidly moving back and soon almost out of sight as the ship continued to on its way. The crew member who had taken charge radioed in and soon the ships engines could be heard throttling down.

Meanwhile the deck hands were attempting to launch the lifeboat. As many nautical disaster victims can attest, launching lifeboats from a ship is never a sure thing and often much more time consuming than one would hope. Many victims of maritime disasters have perished when lifeboat launches were not accomplished in a timely fashion. What seemed like hours passed before the boat was finally lowered into the water. When it was apparent the rescue operation would take much longer to complete, exhausted from a night of revelry and excitement, Ann and I, along with most other passengers retreated to our cabins.

An early riser, around five the next morning I went down to the first deck to see if I could find out what happened. I headed to the area where a crew was now securing the lifeboat back in place. They told me the man in the water had been found around three A.M. He was alive but unconscious and taken to the ship dispensary. Later at breakfast, we found out that the man had only suffered from exposure and would be okay.

That evening was the last night of the cruise and as such, the Captain's Dinner was held. While addressing the gathering, the Captain told us that had the ship been running at speed the man in the water would never have been seen, and in all his years of cruise sailing he had seen less than a half a dozen people pulled out of the water. The man plucked out early that morning was the only one he had ever seen who was alive.

Oh what a lucky man indeed.

Smelt Fishing in Old Kenosha

Many men go fishing all of their lives without knowing that it is not the fish they are after.

Henry David Thoreau

I've gotten some very nice emails and notes regarding my perch fishing story in "Our Wisconsin" magazine. The story, which is also on my blog, recalls those "good old" days on Lake Michigan when we used to catch buckets of yellow perch throughout the spring and summer. Those days, unfortunately, are long gone as Alewives, Zebra and Quagga mussels, along with over fishing have decimated the yellow perch population in Lake Michigan. There is currently a daily limit of five yellow perch on the lake, and truth be told you're often lucky to catch one.

I recently had the opportunity to meet one of my readers and his wife. We had a good time kicking around the old perch fishing days along the Kenosha shoreline. We also talked about those great days in the spring, many years ago when we would catch buckets of smelt which had come in to spawn.

The smelt run would usually start shortly after Easter. The little grunions would be in close to shore for about three weeks before heading back out to deep water for the rest of the year. Fisherman up and down the shores of the great lakes would lay in wait for them, when they would swim in close to shore at night to reproduce.

We'd catch buckets of them!

The Kenosha harbor would be lined up with groups of people using dip nets to catch the tasty little buggers. The dip nets were composed of a large square net on a winch. The net would be lowered to the bottom and cranked up every so often to see if the smelt were "in." Once the smelt were "in" the nets would be cranked up and down frequently and groups of smelt would be scooped out of the net with a smaller dip net. A bright lantern or light was used to see what was in the net, and to also attract the smelt. Dip nets were also used up and down the Kenosha shoreline in the "rocks" but it was not as easy to set-up and sure as heck not as comfortable as smelting on the piers.

It must be mentioned that smelt fishing was the stated reason for going down to the lake and freezing our butts off night after night every spring, however that would not be entirely accurate. Partying…big time partying was as much a part of smelt fishing, if not more than catching the smelt themselves. Vast amounts of alcohol were consumed during the event. Bonfires roared and many portable radios blared out music of one kind or another. Fireworks went off, dogs yelped and yipped and when the run was on, there would be endless yelling and shouting. (On a typical raucous night, several people who fell in would have to be fished out, while on-lookers laughed and cheered.)

Artwork by Lenny Palmer, *see note

Many smelters used a sein net to catch the wily little critters. We had a thirty foot long sein which we would walk out into the lake with. After a short pause, the sein net would go down and we would tap our way back to the shore to hopefully find a net full of smelt. As I was usually the shortest guy in our "crew" I was the pivot man who held onto the net while the taller guy went out into the lake and swung around. Often, especially when the lake was rough, waves would break over our chest waders and we would get a good soaking. As Lake Michigan is never warm, especially on cold spring nights, this is when the alcohol we had consumed, along with our bonfire on shore earned its medal.

Sometimes we'd catch em by the bushel!

There were several locations where we seined in Kenosha—Eichleman Park, Simmons Island next to the north pier, and Barnes Creek in Carol Beach were our favorite spots. Sometimes we'd catch so many smelt that we would drop off buckets of them off at local taverns on our way home. This, of course, was rewarded with many refreshing beverages—and extended the smelt fishing party.

That's great!!

Once home everyone got to work cleaning the smelt. The method to cleaning smelt involved a scissors and your thumb. The smelt would be cut open from the belly to the gills. The guts were squeezed out by inserting the thumb and running it through the length of the open smelt. The smelt cleaning operation often ran well into the next morning, depending on how well we did. Of course, the consumption of various beverages continued during the cleaning procedure and also after wards, as a batch of fresh smelt would be battered and fried.

As with the perch, fried smelt would be served with coleslaw, bread, and the beverage of your choice. Finer dining was never had!!

And, unfortunately the same factors that caused the decline of the lake perch also caused the disappearance of the smelt in the southern portion of Lake Michigan. However as a testament to the popularity of the event, every spring parties are still held at night in many former smelt fishing locations; albeit without the guest of honor... the smelt.

The smelt fishing parties were great!

This article is dedicated to my long time smelt fishing buddies now passed;

Jim Booth, Don Booth and Bob Stevens

Hopefully out there somewhere dipping their nets into the "heavenly waters."

Note: Painting by Lenny Palmer added on 9/15/2019,
Lenny's Artwork may be purchased by contacting him at palmerleonard27@yahoo.com

Mel's Shoes

(Published in MWSA Dispatches Summer 2018)

Sometimes having fun with your best friend is all the therapy you need.

Author Unknown

Introduction

Jim and his wife, Tess

My life long best friend Jim passed away a few years ago. All of us who knew him still miss him very much. In addition to being a good hearted person, Jim was also a constant source of amusement for us all. He had a way of turning a mundane activity into a hilarious adventure. Jim also enjoyed hearing about the adventures he created and laughed as hard as the rest of us whenever they were told and retold. One of Jim's most frequent "victims" over the years was his dad, Mel. This is another story in which Jim provided a hilarious adventure, at poor Mel's expense.

Mel's Shoes

Jim and his family had a cottage on a small lake near Wautoma, Wisconsin. The lake had a nice population of panfish, as well as some nice bass and a few northern pike as well. There were many other lakes and rivers in the area along with a few other attractions, which lured us up there over the years. Jim and I went up there quite a bit in our youth, where we had many fishing and hunting adventures…and a few miss-adventures as well.

Part 2: Outdoor Recreation and Leisure

Jim's cabin in the woods

At one time, some years ago, Jim and I along with his brother Don and his parents Mel and Isla were all up at the cottage at the same time. After an extended rainy period, the yard had become a mud wallow and Mel's boat and trailer sank into the heavy muck. Mel recruited Jim, Don and me to help him get his boat and trailer dislodged from the mud and moved to higher ground.

I looked forward to the task, as any affair involving Jim and his Dad usually turned into a slapstick adventure filled with hilarity.

From an early age, Jim had gotten into the habit of "borrowing" things from his dad, with little or no notice. Jim continued this practice into adulthood.

Mel was a big fellow, quiet but with a wry sense of humor and a keen wit. Over time, Mel, being rather shrewd, implemented a plan to keep track of his possessions and the flow of them. He accomplished this by spray-painting all of his tools and equipment iridescent orange.

Now having done this, any time Mel needed an inventory of his possessions, which he suspected Jim of appropriating, he merely paid Jim a visit and anything with the telltale iridescent orange paint was promptly repossessed.

The plan worked fairly well, however not all of Mel's possessions lent themselves to the garish paint job, and those items that were not suitable for the orange treatment were, unfortunately for Mel, still vulnerable to Jim's predation. A contributing factor in all of this was that as a young adult, Jim was about the same size as Mel.

Now, back to our story regarding the boat and trailer mired in muck. On this particular day, the four of us headed out to rescue Mel's rig, and sure enough, there sat the boat and trailer, buried in about two feet of mud. From where it was located, all we could do was try to push it out by hand, as there was no room for a vehicle on either side.

While Mel and Jim positioned themselves on one side of the boat, Don and I took the other. We were giving it all we had, struggling and pushing it through the muck, while at the same time trying to maintain our balance so as not to end up lying in the wallow alongside the boat. Things were progressing fairly well, and it looked like we would soon get the boat and trailer onto dry ground until Mel suddenly dropped his load and started yelling at the top of his voice

"What the hell are you doing with my new shoes on?" Mel roared. Mel's personal ware was subject to Jim's predation.

Don, Jim and I all looked down, and sure enough, caked in mud though they were, you could clearly see the fine crafted leather of Mel's formerly impeccable new leather dress shoes…on Jim's feet.

Now Jim knew he was in trouble (been there before), and he was soon back peddling as fast as he could, while all the while professing ignorance.

"Dad, I thought they were mine, no kidding…I didn't realize I put your shoes on!"

Red with rage, Mel wasn't buying it, as he went after Jim like a pit bull after a ham bone, yelling and snorting in the process.

Soon Jim was running around the trailer full speed, with a game old Mel hot on his heels. Don and I, now holding up the entire load, and of course laughing like hyenas, finally dropped our load as well.

This hilarious scene went on for a minute or two more until Jim danced far enough away and out of reach, after which Mel just stood and glared at him.

Eventually Mel calmed down and Jim—maintaining his proclamations of innocence—promised to clean the shoes up as good as new, placating Mel just enough. Jim went in the house changed into his own shoes, and returned to position himself at the boat again, making sure to stay out of Mel's reach.

Soon with the boat on dry ground, we all retreated to the cabin, where Jim spent the better part of an hour cleaning Mel's new shoes…under the watchful eye of Mel of course.

Jim's motto was "if the shoe fits... wear it."

NOTE: Although Jim borrowed some of my "stuff" over the years, as I borrowed some of his, I never had to worry about him borrowing my clothing or foot wear. Jim was 6'2" tall and had enormous hands and feet. He wore a size fourteen shoe, compared to my size eight.

On more than one occasion I complained about having to pay the same amount for my shoes as he did for his, despite the difference in size. "Yours take half a cow," I would say.

Bald at an early age, Jim would respond by pointing out that he and I paid the same amount for a haircut. Case closed!

THE FIRE

Published by the MWSA 2017 spring edition

Camping is six month's worth of adventure, packed into a weekend.

Joe

Our tent camping days were over!

Some years ago my wife Ann and I decided to buy a recreational camper. Although we had tent camped early in our marriage, for many years, along with our children, we stayed at remote cabins in Northern Wisconsin in order to get that great outdoors experience. We fished, swam, boated, and immersed ourselves in nature; but now our children had grown and we missed getting out in the wild. We felt camping would fill that void.

With a modest budget we set out to find a camper which would satisfy our needs. We visited an RV dealer in the area to see what they had available. Their showroom and lot included a variety of campers, both large and small. Some included every creature comfort one could ask for, others were a bit more Spartan, but still a step up from our old tent camping days.

After disclosing our budget, (I'm cheap) the dealer got a sour look on his face and directed us to the back of the lot where their "pre-owned" inventory resided. There we found a group of older camping units in various conditions.

The one that best fit our intended outlay (did I mention that I'm cheap?) was a very large 1970s era truck camper fixed upon a 1984 GMC heavy duty pick-up truck. The vintage unit, stood like a hulking mammoth amongst the newer more streamlined campers in the lot; faded paint and rust tarnishing its once, no doubt, sparkling image. The truck itself was powered by a three hundred and fifty cubic inch engine with a four barrel carburetor. It was equipped with two twenty six gallon fuel tanks, oversized steel belted tires, and an extra-large capacity radiator; it oozed raw power. Secured to this mighty beast was the vintage camper itself, which slept four. (Five if they were friendly) It contained a queen size bed, a fold out twin bed, a small stove, refrigerator, furnace, forty gallon water tank and two forty gallon propane tanks. It had a small bathroom with a toilet and sink; the shower spigot was affixed to the exterior of the unit, which for the more tepid camper may have compromised any sense of privacy, not to mention leaving the bather at the mercy of the elements.

Our dog's reservation aside, we were happy with our purchase.

And although the interior décor was straight off the set of the Brady Bunch; just as Ralphie dreamt about his bb gun on *A Christmas Story*, I was smitten by this hulking conveyance from campgrounds of yesteryear. A deal was struck and soon we were pulling our magnificent, though admittedly seasoned, home on wheels into our driveway. I had to creep ever so slowly up to the garage as the top of the camper exceeded that of the gutters on our house. The width of the behemoth forced me to disassemble our back fence and gate in order to get it through. And although I had driven slow enough to gain some of the neighbor's attention, the looks they gave were not exactly the looks of envy and admiration I had hoped for. I chalked it off as jealousy or ignorance regarding the wonderful world of RV camping, which we had now entered.

After showing off our new toy to anyone who got near our house, we scheduled a weekend camping trip at a public campground not too far from home. This would be our shake-down cruise where we would both learn how (if) everything worked, and get acquainted with the finer nuances of (semi) modern camping. The trip went well, other than taking out a gutter and a few tree branches, no major disasters occurred and as I was untested regarding the dreaded "black water" disposal procedure I insisted that all necessary bathroom trips be made

at the public restrooms the campground featured. My order was ignored by us both during the middle of the night, forcing me to use the on-site disposal facility before we left; an extremely unpleasant experience in every way. (Reference the movie RV)

Satisfied with our maiden voyage, the camper soon found itself on a cross country trip to the east coast. My good friend Tim, who I served in Vietnam with, suggested we make a pilgrimage to the Vietnam War memorial in Washington D.C. So off I went, to pick up Tim and a friend of his in Ohio before traveling on to D.C. However after spending not one full day on the trip, Tim's friend decided that traveling in a cramped truck cab was not his cup of tea and bailed, leaving Tim and I to make (and fund) the voyage on our own.

The trip went along fine, until we hit some rain and fog while driving at night through some mountains west of Washington D.C. The clearance between the side of the mountain and our lumbering camper was so slight I thought we'd surely scrape the remaining paint off of the vehicle while getting through. Things took a serious turn for the worse when our windshield wipers stopped working. Of course, there were no exits until we cleared the area, and had there been any I wouldn't have been able to see them anyway.

We survived the white knuckle drive and made it to a campground where we slept and managed to replace the windshield wiper motor the next morning. We then proceeded to a campground outside of D.C. where we stayed for two days. We took a commuter bus into Washington D.C. itself where we visited Arlington National Cemetery, The Vietnam War Memorial, and several other attractions. The trip home was uneventful and quiet as we were immersed in our own thoughts regarding our visit to the Wall. (And the logic of taking a vehicle that gets seven miles to the gallon on a cross-country trip)

Gas mileage aside, with a successful voyage under its belt, Ann and I felt that our camping unit, albeit costly to operate, had proven its mettle and we soon prepared for another trip. We planned on going to a small campground in Central Wisconsin about four hours from home. The campground was on a lake with a nice population of fish so we hooked up our small boat to tow behind the camper. Looking forward to our trip, we left early in the morning on the fourth of July, equipped for a five day stay. Packed with food, clothing, fishing gear and supplies we got out on the highway and headed north. It was a hot day so we had the air-conditioner going full blast. The trip went smoothly for the first couple of hours. Being the fourth of July, the roads were packed with holiday travelers. With a full load and towing a boat, we stayed in the right hand lane.

At around the half way point to our destination the temperature gauge on the truck pegged *dead hot.* Alarmed, I pulled over on the shoulder and popped the hood. You could have roasted a pig on the engine block as waves of searing heat emanated from it. I gave the engine about fifteen minutes to cool, then drove along the shoulder and pulled off at the next exit. Luckily there was a truck stop with a full garage right at the intersection. I pulled in, and although the mechanic was ready to close for the holiday he agreed to work on the truck. After checking it out, he said the serpentine belt was shot and it would take about an hour to change. I gave him the go ahead and we waited.

When the repair was done, we topped off the two gas tanks (yeah; seven miles to the gallon) and got back on the highway. However we didn't get five miles before the temperature gauge pegged *dead hot again*! I let go with a few nice expletives, pulled over on the shoulder and popped the hood… but this time all hell broke loose.

Huge, bright flames leapt from the engine compartment on all three sides of the open hood, some reaching four or five feet in the air. For several seconds Ann and I just stared in astonishment. Coming to our senses I yelled at Ann to get out of the truck. As she grabbed her purse and opened the door I pushed her out, ran around to her side and ushered her back about twenty feet behind the truck. I told her to stay put and ran back. Flames now engulfed the entire front of the truck including the cab that we had occupied just seconds earlier. I opened the back of the camper to see if there was anything I could save, but the fire now burned through and through and I was driven back by the heat. I did manage to get some fishing tackle out of the boat (priorities) but soon even there the heat was too intense so I had to retreat back to where Ann was standing along with a few good Samaritans who had pulled over. One of them had a cell phone and called the fire in. We then stood watching helplessly as the holiday traffic slowly motored past our burning rig, gaping at the ever increasing fire.

Soon a state trooper arrived and after assessing the situation started directing traffic into the far left lane, as flames were now encroaching into the right lane. Being in a rural area, the first volunteer fire department arrived shortly after. The fireman in charge stared in astonishment at the *huge fireball*, now raging on the side of the road. Obviously anticipating a small engine fire, he hurriedly radioed in for more help. Within the next half hour several more volunteer fire units arrived, and try though they may, they could neither put out, nor slow the fire down for quite some time.

Fueled by 52 gallons of gasoline, 80 gallons of propane, four oversize steel belted radials, and untold other flammable odds and ends, the *fire was so intense* the four state troopers now on hand closed all lanes of the northbound highway. The grass between the northbound and southbound highway as well as the shoulder ignited from the heat, forcing some of the firefighters to tend to those areas.

In addition, the black top underneath the burning vehicles melted and caught on fire as well, spreading along the road like a snake diverting yet more firefighters. Adding to the din, cement in the lane next to the shoulder started fracturing from the heat.

We provided entertainment for the holiday crowd.

As all of this was taking place, Ann stayed back watching in horror. I hopped back and forth between the various firefighters and police, trying in some way to help and also to convince them not to take any unnecessary risks attempting to save anything. The last thing I wanted was to see anyone get hurt trying to salvage our less than prime camper, truck and fishing boat.

My requests to the firefighters fell on deaf ears, as they continually moved closer and closer to the *raging inferno* while applying water and chemicals. One of the state troopers on hand advised me that these people lived for events like this and to just sit back and let them have their fun. I was OK with that until one of the firefighters had to be placed in the rescue squad as a result of heat exhaustion. That bothered me considerably, as I felt it was unnecessary. (And I was worried just a little bit that I might be held liable)

In the meantime, passersby were putting on their own show. Northbound traffic was closed completely for almost one hour until the blaze was under control. Many holiday travelers, unhappy at having their vacations delayed, yelled obscenities or communicated their displeasure with a hand gesture. I sheepishly grinned and ignored them in most cases; in other cases I yelled back or returned the offensive gesture.

Other people were more understanding, giving us looks of sympathy or shouts of encouragement. One of the firefighting team members on hand was a grievance councilor who stayed with Ann during most of the ordeal. (Before therapy puppies and hot cocoa were in vogue) Attempting to show a brave face, Ann told the firefighters that the ribs in the freezer were probably done by now and they could have them for dinner.

As the **huge tires burned**, the sky became blackened with thick, acrid smoke. It turned the early-afternoon sky black and hindered the camera activity of the news chopper which kept circling overhead trying to film the event. (He was probably flashing that same hand gesture)

Within three hours, but what seemed like forever to us, the fire was out and all that remained was the charred hull and powertrain of the truck, the boat trailer, anchor and the little Smoky Joe Weber grill; minus handle and hardware which had burned up along with everything else in our possession. The boat and camper itself, along with our clothing, fishing tackle, household goods, personal items, food, beverages, tools, etc., were "gone with the wind." Now, as if on cue, every person on site stood still and took stock of the situation. And in one last bit of triumph for the Gods of fire, the Smoky Joe Grill, which evidently had been building up with heat pressure, blew. The top half of the sphere went **screaming straight up into the air** about forty feet. As everyone watched, gravity finally took over and it fell back to earth right in the midst of everyone, landing with a bang, still spinning for another twenty seconds, like a dime tossed on a steel plate. That was the coup de gras, after which everyone on hand, Ann and I included, laughed and cheered. Exhausted firefighters now sat and relaxed, a few troopers started leaving and traffic was freed up to go on its way.

A large wrecker with a flatbed trailer arrived and the skeletal remains of our truck, camper and boat trailer were loaded on and taken to a nearby service center. The firefighter with heat exhaustion had recovered, we thanked everyone on hand and said goodbye; they said goodbye in return and wished us luck. One of the troopers drove us to the service center where our burnt out wreck was now on display for anyone in the area to gape at.

Our son Billy and his girlfriend at the time, (now wife) Jessica; visiting on one of our camping trips.

After filling out paperwork, we phoned our son Billy in Milwaukee and gave him a brief explanation of what happened. He immediately left to come and get us. Now with idle time on our hands we drank liquids and consoled each other over our loss; while passersby stopped and gawked at the charred remains of our property.

Our son Billy and his girlfriend at the time, (now wife) Jessica, visiting on one of our camping trips.

When Billy arrived, he pulled into the lot and slowly got out of his car, staring incredulously at the burnt out remains of our once fine truck, camper and boat. The boat and camper had burnt up completely with no visible remains. What did remain from the fire, the hull of the truck, drivetrain and boat trailer, sat discolored and warped, seemingly naked and exposed to the world. From the earlier phone conversation, Billy had gotten the impression that there was just a small engine fire and the vehicle would be repaired and picked up at a later date. Now he stood in shock, staring back and forth at the skeletal remains of our rig and then at us. Ann, watching Billie's reaction, now started sobbing. I walked over to him and cracked a few jokes; "You should see the other guy" and things of that nature. He just kept shaking his head in amazement. We touched base with the shop manager who told us there would be some reports and a scrap charge he would send us, whereupon we left. The trip home was fairly quiet, with all of us numb, so small talk was pretty much out.

After the ordeal we were relieved to get home to a familiar and safe environment. Being the fourth of July, Billy had plans for the evening so he headed back to Milwaukee. We thanked him for his help and somewhat sadly watched him leave. We called our insurer and left a message on their voicemail. Our daughter JoAnn was in California at the time and we decided to tell her when she returned so as not to ruin her trip. Ann called her sister who was having a fourth of July party at her house. She suggested we stop by to try and salvage the rest of the day. When we got there, of course, we had to retell the story, to everyone's amazement. But we did manage to relax a little and had a pretty good time and a couple of good laughs regarding the whole episode. Later everyone was glued to the television as our catastrophe made the six o'clock news out of Milwaukee. The aerial film was of poor quality, with smoke from the fire the only thing visible, so it was just a short blurb.

The next week was hectic with calls back and forth to our insurer, the state patrol and the towing company. We also had to go on several shopping sprees as much of our personal property had been consumed by the fire. This made Ann happier and me unhappier. (For months and even a few years after, we would be looking for something and then suddenly remember "oh yeah, that was lost in the fire")

The nice little camper we got after the fire.

Fortunately we had replacement insurance on our vehicle and personal property, so I was eventually able to replace the truck, camper and boat...with an upgrade in each case. And as I expected, when everything was clear and done, the insurance company canceled our policy faster than Oliver Hardy taking down a cream puff.

The 36 foot rig we had prior to the mobile home. (our "long, long trailer")

Despite our disaster, Ann and I kept right on camping. With our new (used) travel trailer pulled behind our new (used) pick-up truck we had many fine camping excursions with our children and friends. We've had a couple other rigs since then as well. Today we have an old mobile home near a lake in Central Wisconsin where we spend much of our time. We don't have to tow it, level it, flush out any waste tanks or even wash it.

We do, however, have to make sure IT DOESN'T BURN TO THE GROUND!

The mobile home we currently have in Central Wisconsin.

A nice 26 Jayco we had near Corpus Christi, Texas for a time.

Tommy and the Turtle

Fishing with Tommy is a hoot!

Joe

My friend Tommy and I have had many great fishing adventures over the years. We've ice fished, river fished, pond fished, fished in the big water of Lake Michigan and the far northern reaches of Canada. Tom, originally from Denmark, was a Merchant Marine, then a plumber and is an overall very good natured dude. Among his many talents, Tom makes great homemade wine, which he refers to as lunker juice.

Tommy with a nice walleye he caught on our Canadian fishing trip not too long ago.

Several years ago, Tommy and I were fishing near a dam along the banks of the Fox River in Central Wisconsin, where I have a nearby mobile home. Tommy was fishing right up by the dam itself, casting for walleyes. I was downstream a bit and one other fisherman was in between us.

I was catching a few catfish here and there, and wasn't aware of how Tommy was doing. However after a short time, I noticed him bringing in a nice fish, although I didn't know what it was. Soon Tommy yelled for me to come and check out the nice walleye he had caught.

Being as I had already lost two poles in that body of water to wily catfish dragging my unattended rig in, I pulled both rods out of the water and went to check out Tom's catch.

Tom had put the fish on a stringer and left it in the river to stay fresh, however when he tried to bring the stringer in he encountered unexpected resistance. "What the heck" Tom said, needing both hands to pull the stringer up out of the water.

Sure enough, now out of the water at the end of the stringer was his nice walleye…with a very large snapping turtle hanging on to its tail!

Normally very easy going, Tom's a hoot when he's stirred up! Now glaring at the fish snatching snapper he starts yelling and cussing and shaking the stringer in attempt to dislodge the interloper. "Sonofgun let go of my walleye you damn snapper!" These and other fine words were showered upon the unwelcome beast.

Finally after a time, the snapper released the fish, dropped to the ground; and went after Tommy's foot like a pit bull after a ham bone. "Cod darn you, you sonofagun" …along with another string of fine epitaphs poured from Tommy's mouth as he danced and dodged on the steep little bank in an effort to evade the bite of the hard shelled terrorist.

By now, the other fisherman and I were laughing so hard we could barely stand, so we weren't much help at all.

After a struggle, Tommy managed to get his foot under the snapper's shell and kick him back into the river. Shaking his fist, finally victorious, Tommy proceeded to assess the damage the turtle inflicted on his prize catch.

The other fisherman, still laughing, now commented, "Where's a darn video camera when you need one?"

Tom filleted his nice walleye and took it home. And during those times while enjoying "lunker juice" and telling stories, Tom takes the ribbing about his run-in with the turtle terrorist with good humor.

Section 3

WORK & LIFE

In addition to those previously described in this book, Joe has had many interesting experiences in life in general. Here are a few.

The Paper Route

Published in Happenings Magazine Smart Reader
1/14/2021

With Christmas tips in my pocket, I felt like Rockefeller.

Joe

Growing up in Kenosha back in the fifties and sixties, many of us boys (and a few girls) had a paper route by the time we were twelve years old. Our allowances pretty much expired by that age, and our fathers let us know it was time to start earning our own spending money. (And they weren't too subtle about it either)

The premier paper route job in Kenosha was that of a Kenosha News carrier. The Kenosha News routes were thought to be gravy jobs, because most of the people in Kenosha got that paper and as a result, the route sizes were small, but concentrated. You could walk those routes easily in an hour or so. If you had a Kenosha News route, you were high on the pecking order as a kid.

The other type of paper route to be had in Kenosha was a Henoch News agency route. These routes delivered the Chicago Tribune, Chicago Sun Times, Chicago American, Milwaukee Journal and Milwaukee Sentinel. Customers for those papers were much fewer and farther between, so the routes were large and spread out. Each of these papers was larger than the Kenosha News and required folding the various sections together before delivery. Because of the large spread and size of the routes, it typically took at least two hours to complete the route, sometimes three. The highly valued Kenosha News routes were handed down from family member to family member, so we ended up with a Henoch route.

My brother John and I started out with a Sunday route, and kept that going for a couple of years. Later, we got a daily route which paid more. When we first started out, we had to collect the money from the customers, and that would take another two to three hours each week. Henoch News eventually came up with a collection system that eliminated the need for the carrier to collect from the customer. That saved time, but also cut us out on many of the weekly tips we may have gotten. (At Christmas time, using cheap calendars as bait, we lobbied for tips)

Spring, summer and fall weren't too bad as far as delivering papers in Kenosha. But winter…winter added a whole new set of problems to the task. My brother and I both had bicycles with side baskets which would hold many papers. Two or three trips to refill and we'd be done. In the winter, when the weather was bad, we had three choices; talk "Dad" into driving us, walk the route with newspaper bags, or use the sled with a special box for carrying loads. You can guess how much luck we had convincing Dad to take us. Walking our routes with the bag or the sled added at least two hours to our delivery time, but you do what you have to do. In the spring, summer and fall, rainy days presented problems as well. The newspapers were dropped off in bulk in front of our house in the early morning. If it was raining, we'd end up with a bundle of soggy newspapers.

Bad weather wasn't the only problem we encountered during our paper route days. In the days when we still had to collect from the customers, there were always customers who we had to call on several times before we could collect the money owed. Occasionally the news agency would tire of their stalling and cancel their subscription.

Newspaper carriers and mail carriers both had to deal with a common enemy on occasion…dogs. Loose dogs would sometimes threaten us and even chase us off our routes. We got pretty adept at whacking them with a rolled-up newspaper while pedaling away as fast as we could.

One dog of note, harassed me on my route for a couple of months one year. I complained to the owners and the news agency but nothing helped. My mother didn't like dogs, so we never had one. But now and then I'd bring home a stray and she'd let me keep it for a short while.

One of the strays I adopted solved the problem of the constant harassment I had been getting from the dog on my route. This particular stray was a large Boxer. I started taking it on my route, with the leash attached to the handle bars on my bicycle. Sure enough, one day the dog that had been harassing me came tearing out after us. I let the boxer off the leash and he taught that dog a well-deserved lesson. I had to give up the boxer after a couple of weeks, but was never harassed by the other dog again!

Despite a few inconveniences' and problems on our various paper routes, I mostly enjoyed them and picked up enough money to carry me along for three or four years.

The Nicklaus Gears

Sometimes good material just presents itself.

Joe

I've met my share of celebrities over the years. Living in Southern California for a time, as well as a life of travel seems to have brought me my share of opportunities in rubbing up against some of the rich and famous.

I met Elvis Presley in 1971 in Dick Dale's bar outside of Riverside, California. Elvis and Dick Dale were friends and he happened to be in the small bar the only time I ever went there. He shook my hand and gave me a "Hey, how ya doin." When I tell people about that encounter some are flabbergasted and ask for MY autograph!

I met Jesse Jackson in, of all places, Copenhagen, Denmark in 1996. I was on a business trip for the company I worked for at the time and Jesse was at an international symposium for humanity…or some such conference. We were staying at the same hotel and I bumped into him in front of the hotel when I was returning from some night entertainment. I introduced myself and told him I was from Kenosha, Wisconsin, just north of Chicago. "Wisconsin…I know where that is," Jesse said as he shook my hand.

I also met Susan St. James, Artie Johnson, Little Richard, Joe Louis and a few other celebrities of note, and some of not so note. The recent passing of Arnold Palmer brought to mind my encounter with his good friend and golfing buddy, Jack Nicklaus.

Some years ago I worked for a company called Jacobsen Textron. Jacobsen was in the business of making turf care equipment. They specialized in servicing the golf industry. One piece of equipment they offered was a small utility vehicle for use on golf courses. A problem with the utility vehicle surfaced when Jack Nicklaus called. The vehicle was designed for power, and as such was robust—but noisy. Nicklaus reported that golfers on the courses he was involved with were complaining about the excess noise. A team at Jacobsen was formed to address the problem. I was assigned to the team to represent the purchasing department, which was responsible for the procurement of all purchased components for the vehicle—the gears being among them.

The problem turned out to be an engineering design. The gears on the vehicle used a common straight or spur gear set, which although robust, transmitted a significant amount of noise. The engineers on the team designed a new gear train which used helical gears. Helical gears were strong, quiet...and costly to manufacture. The supplier was given the new design and came back with a long lead time for delivery of the new gears. The orders were placed and management was advised of the status.

Not more than a couple of weeks passed before Jack Nicklaus called the president of Jacobsen, Dick Miller. The two were casual acquaintances as a result of their business interaction. Nicklaus wanted to know when those new gears for the utility cart would be ready. Miller told him it would be several months, but promised to do everything he could to get the product in as soon as possible.

This did not placate Nicklaus for long, as he was soon calling on a weekly basis. On one particular day, Dick Miller had enough. He told Nicklaus he could speak directly to the person responsible for the purchase of those gears. Sitting in my cubical at the time I answered the ringing phone.

"Is this Joe Campolo?"

"Yes, may I help you?" I asked.

"This is Jack Nicklaus. When the hell are we gonna get those new gears for the utility cart?"

Pausing for a second, I suspected one of my department buddies was pranking me as we had been known to do from time to time. "Bernie?" I asked.

From the phone, "Who's Bernie?"

I wasn't convinced. "Bernie, don't mess with me."

Now another voice, "Joe, this is Dick Miller. Jack here would like to know what we can do to get those darn utility cart gears in quicker."

Recognizing Dick Miller's voice, I stammered a bit. "Uh, well, we've been pounding on the vendor pretty good, but let me call again today and see if I can hold their feet to the fire a bit."

Nicklaus jumped back in, "That would be great Joe, see what you can do. Dick, keep me posted on this."

"Will do, Jack. Joe, call me as soon as you get an answer."

I informed the head of our department of the call from Miller and Nicklaus and we then called the gear manufacturer. We explained the circumstances and they got a pretty good kick out of it.

"For Jack Nicklaus, we will cut the lead time down to four weeks." They told us.

We didn't call Dick Miller back right away however—we waited until the next afternoon. We didn't want him to think it was that easy, otherwise pulling rabbits out of hats would be expected on a regular basis. When we did call, he was pretty happy. We got a few nice "att-a- boys" out of it and the utility cart gears were henceforth known far and wide as the "Nicklaus gears."

P.S. I'm a lousy golfer

Chaos and Creativity: The Sixties and Seventies

We are each given an infinitesimal chance at the universe; what will we do with that chance?

Joe

The Sixties are Forever on Our Mind

We hear much about the cataclysmic events of the sixties, hardly a day goes by without the airing of a TV program depicting the chaotic events of those years. The War in Vietnam and the Civil Rights movement are fought and refought every day on cable TV, the Internet, and whatever is left of our printed media industry.

Though seldom acknowledged as such, the period starting in the early sixties and ending in the late seventies was one of the most productive periods in our nation's history, from a creativity standpoint. Advancements in science and technology, spiked in almost direct proportion to the escalating violence on our streets and in the steaming jungles, fields and mountains of Vietnam. And along with that spike in science and technology a burst of creative activity also occurred in the arts, including literature, film and music.

Surges of Creativity throughout History

All through history there have been periods of explosive creativity, peppered over the eons. At various times down through the years rapid creativity has changed and enhanced the condition of man. Man's major advancements have not typically occurred in an orderly, sequential fashion, but rather they have occurred in great spurts here and there down through time.

Roman Creativity Transformed the World

Ancient Greece and Rome were considered to be two of the most creative empires in history. Each of these dynasties fueled rapid advancements in  warfare, technology, art and literature, throughout their tenure. And much of that activity happened in short ten to twenty-year spurts. Some ancient Chinese dynasties experienced creative activity in much the same fashion.

After the fall of Rome, the world slept for several centuries before awakening again during the Renaissance. Centered in Italy, the arts, literature, architecture and music once more sprang to life. Advances in the various sciences soon followed. All of this advancement ultimately led to the great age of exploration highlighted by the discoveries in the new world.

Roman creativity transformed the world

In the 17th Century, Louis the Sun King prodded France into leading the world in creativity during that time. The Age of Enlightenment followed soon after.

Another great creative boom came in the late 1800s and lasted into the 1920s. Electricity, radio, automobiles, airplanes and many other inventions ushered in the 20th century. The continual state of warfare in the late 1800s and on well into the 1900s compressed and accelerated the rapid expansion of ideas regarding science, technical fields and the arts as well. As peoples struggled with the cloak of war constantly over their head like the sword of Damocles, the world responded with a dynamic expansion of literature, visual art, music and then film. This creativity continued throughout much of the 20th century.

World War I and particularly World War II provided the world with many new technological marvels. Not just in the field of weaponry, as significant gains in the medical field were made as well. The horrors of the wars were expressed on canvas, as artwork reflecting the condition of man became popular. Vast amounts of new literature were penned by authors, old and new. Music, listened to by bored and cash strapped citizens and soldiers became cheap entertainment for the masses.

Space, War, the Arts and Rock & Roll

Starting in the late 1950s and continuing into the late 1970s yet another period of explosive creativity ensued. Space exploration and war, fueled by competition between the two super powers, the U.S.S.R. and the U.S.A., spurred tremendous scientific and technological advancement. Though intended for war and exploration rather than the betterment of man, advances made during this period also improved, if not complicated the lives of man. Computers, automation and rapid communication sprung up all over the civilized world.

THE SIXTIES AND SEVENTIES EXPLODE ON THE SCENE

If a creativity graph of the sixties and seventies were made it would show a gently rising curve during the early sixties followed by huge jumps from the mid-sixties to the mid-seventies, and then a gentle tapering off. The growth of creativity during that time seemed to crest during the later years of the Vietnam War, and decline after the end of the war. Perhaps coincidental, perhaps not.

Technological and scientific advances during that time were most evident in the space race, climaxing with the moon landing in 1969. When John F. Kennedy pressed the Moon button in 1962, he also opened the bank for vast amounts of research and exploration. And all kinds of stuff came out of those programs; microchips, computers, memory foam and new food preservatives, to name just a few. (Tang was actually developed before the space race)

> CHANGE IS THE LAW OF LIFE.
>
> AND THOSE WHO LOOK ONLY TO THE PAST OR PRESENT ARE SURE TO MISS THE FUTURE.
>
> -JOHN F. KENNEDY

Nixon with Apollo astronauts.

Literature Led the Way

Steinbeck

Great literature ushered in the sixties. Monumental authors like Steinbeck and Hemingway had earlier produced great works of literature, whose popularity resurged in the sixties.

Steinbeck

Kerouac

Newer authors including Harper Lee, Joseph Heller, Hunter Thompson and many others wrote books which tied into the counterculture and the essence of those years. Germain Greer, Charles Bukowski, Allen Ginsberg, James Arthur Baldwin, Alexander Solzhenitsyn and the works of Jack Kerouac also helped define the decade. It would be impossible to list all of the important works of literature and authors from those days when everything was questioned and seemingly up for grabs.

Important works of literature continued to spring up on into the seventies. Authors such as John Updike, Joseph Wambaugh, and E.L. Doctorow to name a few produced great written pieces. Kurt Vonnegut, Alex Haley, Tom Wolfe and Gloria Steinem wrote works significant to the time as well. New authors such as Stephen King, David Reuben, Carl Bernstein, Robert Woodward and Mario Puzo added to the list. As with the sixties, it would be difficult to list all of the authors who had an impact during that time. As a writer and an avid reader, it was seldom that I was not in the middle of one or two very good books during those years.

The Film Industry migrates along with Literature

As the television and motion picture industry caught up with literature, the nature of the medium transformed as the Sixties moved along. From The Sound of Music to Hair, from The Apartment to In The Heat of the Night, from Tom Jones to In Cold Blood, the big screen became angrier and edgier.

With the six o'clock news constantly bearing grim stories and films of war and civil disturbances, viewers yearned for an escape. TV shows like The Twilight Zone, The Outer Limits, and One Step Beyond sent people on a fantasy tour where they could see crazier things than the reality they lived in and allowed them to fantasize about other worlds. Star Trek became hugely popular, the script often reflecting philosophical themes of the day.

Kerouac

In 1971 All In The Family debuted, pitting old conservative philosophy against young liberal thinking. Various imitations of the show popped up over the next several years, with mixed success. In one of the most watched episodes of All In The Family, a young draft dodger and an older man whose son had been killed in Vietnam found themselves together at the Bunker home for a holiday meal. Despite Archie's discomfort, the older man revealed that he felt that the young draft dodger was correct in his position on the war, much to the chagrin of Archie of course.

Did the times define the music, or the music define the times?

Most of the music stations on my Sirius radio subscription play music from the sixties and seventies. Seldom do I drive anywhere when I am not listening to some of those great old tunes. My children also enjoy the music from those days, and I have no doubt my grandchildren will also, when they come of age.

And I liked it all: Folk, Rock, Soul, Country, Rockabilly and funk. Coming in with a bang, stars like Elvis, Jerry Lee Lewis, Johnny Cash and others ushered

Rock and Rockabilly into the Sixties. Folk singers like The Kingston Trio gave way to Peter Paul & Mary, who in turn gave way to Dylan and Joan Baez. Pete Seeger and Phil Ochs carried on for Woodie Guthrie who died in 1961. Folk music, it was said, held the pulse of America.

The so called "British Invasion" including The Beatles, The Rolling Stones, Dusty Springfield and many others made a huge and lasting impression on Rock & Roll in America.

Like many others, the Beatles also evolved.

And in America hundreds of it's own citizens were cranking out great tunes as well. We listened to them in junior high school, high school, college, at work and of course, in the military. In Vietnam, Radio Saigon was on every minute we could listen. And those that had portable radios or stereos in the larger base camps, naval ships and airbases played their favorite tunes whenever they could. "Good Morning Vietnam" coined by the late Adrian Cronauer could be heard all over Vietnam every morning, through rain, shine, mortar attack, fire fight or quiet time.

Part 3: Work and Life

The War changed everything.

As times grew more acrimonious in the late sixties, the music did as well. The softer melodic tones heard earlier in the decade, tempered by the war in Vietnam, the civil rights movement and the world-wide counterculture movement turned harsh and angry. Hard rock and acid rock ascended, as did an angrier soul and funk. The music reflected the times; impatient, impertinent and in your face. Creedance Clearwater Revival, Janis Joplin, Jimmy Hendrix, Otis Redding, Wilson Picket and many other heavy jamsters pounded the airwaves.

Eventually the war in Vietnam tapered down and finally ended, the civil rights movement reached appeasement, and the world counterculture movement passed. Thus…the music changed again. Softer rock, Pop rock, various Country & Western music and finally Disco arrived on the scene. Music had migrated from the political turmoil of the sixties and early seventies back to more subdued tunes all around the country. As the bombing in Southeast Asia ceased along with the military draft, the harsh and angry music spawned by the war, withered away with it.

THE CREATIVE LEGACY OF THE SIXTIES AND SEVENTIES

With the counterculture dried up along with the war in Vietnam, Americans now pursued other interests and activities. The movement had faded away. Film makers got a lot of mileage out of the war, creating many Vietnam War related films and even a few television shows. Many books have been written about those events.

The surge of musical creativity seen in the sixties and seventies, however, tapered off dramatically. With the exception of rap, few new expressions of music have come out in the ensuing years. And nothing has come close to achieving the impact of the rock movement from those two turbulent decades.

The advent of the Internet, crossing into mainstream society during the nineteen nineties, is yet another form of creativity, impacting many aspects of human life. The creative nature of man will never cease.

The Emperor of the North Pole

Show me an alley, show me a train. Show me a hobo who sleeps out in the rain. And I'll show you a young man with many reasons why, there but for fortune, go you or I.

Phil Ochs

I had quite a few jobs when I was a kid, delivering newspapers, washing windows, all the usual stuff. However one job I had when I was around fifteen stands out.

In my hometown of Kenosha, Wisconsin the Becker brothers had three small sundry stores scattered around town. Very small by today's standards they were called "Becker's Cigar Store" and they offered, beer, magazines, watches, some five and dime type items, and of course, tobacco products of all kinds.

My dad knew the Becker boys from way back and managed to get me a job at the store located by the train station near downtown. (not the best neighborhood in town)

For $1.10/hour I waited on trade, washed the floors, stocked shelves and closed up at night. It was a one man operation, so the shift could be long and boring. And even though I was only fifteen, I sold beer and was expected to check ID's and enforce the law regarding underage purchases . Of course, many of my friends and acquaintances made a bee line to the place in an attempt to procure beer. And yes, I have to admit at times I was persuaded to sell it to them. (times were different back then)

One very entertaining aspect of the job for me, was watching the tramps jumping on and off the trains coming in and out. Some, off the inbound trains, would wander over to the store and panhandle. I usually gave them a free coffee and bag of potato chips. They'd soon turn the coffee into a milkshake, loading it up with cream and sugar.

One particularly charismatic tramp would tell stories which I, along with the other tramps and anyone else in the store would listen to. He spun all kinds of  exciting tales involving railroad detectives, bad weather, and fortunes won and lost. He claimed he was a personal friend of the "Emperor of the North Pole" who he supposedly was befriended by in his "early" years riding the rails. He was quite entertaining.

Unfortunately my job at Beckers was to come to a sudden end one day. I was alone in the store, as usual, when two large men came in. One produced a very large switchblade and told me to "just be cool." They came around the counter and filled two large bags with watches, and other products from the display case. Strangely they didn't ask me to open the cash register, and I never really felt threatened by them. When their sacks were full, they just smiled and left. The next day, when my mother found out, she insisted I quit the job.

But I often think about those days watching the trains coming in and out, wondering about where they were coming and going…and I also think about the wily cast of characters who went in and out with them.

THE PALOMINO CLUB

Appreciation is a wonderful thing: It makes what is excellent in others belong to us as well.

Voltaire

Recently I came upon a Facebook page for The Palomino, a night club that was located in North Hollywood, California. I was sad to hear that The Palomino had closed back in 1995.

In the early seventies after my military service had ended, I lived in North Hollywood for a time. I stayed with friends and relatives until I got a job, after which I moved to the Olive Tree apartments on Lankershim Boulevard which was just down the street from The Palomino.

Buck Owens—a fixture at The Palomino

The Palomino was in its heyday back then, and although primarily a country western club, they also featured various rock and roll entertainers as well. Buck Owens often played at The Palomino and being within earshot while out by our swimming pool and deck, we'd often here "It's Cryin Time Again" by Buck and his Buckaroos. The Palomino's music made for a festive atmosphere at our apartment building and many people visited us just to listen to the Palomino's music.

In the spring of 1973 a strong earthquake hit the San Fernando Valley where North Hollywood is located. By then I had been through many earthquakes and tremors including the powerful Sylmar earthquake which happened on my first morning in California in 1971. In 1971, having just returned from Vietnam, I woke up thinking we were under a Vietcong mortar and rocket attack; until I shook off the cobwebs and remembered I was no longer in Vietnam. That was indeed a rude awakening to California for me.

The earthquake in '73 was not as severe as the Sylmar quake which was a huge jolting quake. The '73 quake was rather a large rolling quake. I had just made my morning coffee preparing to go to work when it hit. I temporarily lost my balance and lay down on the floor till it was over. I then went outside where a chaotic scene was playing out. People from all the apartments were out there, clamoring around in their underwear, excitedly jabbering about the quake. Many streets were closed because of broken utility lines and water pipes so we all got a bonus day off. We quickly turned the event into an all apartment party and had a helluva good time. When our supplies of liquid refreshments ran out, The Palomino and other nearby establishments were visited and depleted of their supplies.

Damage from the Sylmar quake of 1971.

Later that day I received word from my employer that the building had been damaged in the quake and deemed uninhabitable until it could be repaired. Clueless, I initially celebrated the news that would extend me for weeks without a paycheck. Soon, my paltry savings dried up and I found myself in a financial bind. My great Aunt and other relatives and friends let me know I could have meals with them and even move back if need be, but I had a tough time swallowing my pride and determined to tough it out.

It wasn't long before I was hard pressed. With the rent overdue, I took to climbing in through the bathroom window (yep, just like in the song) to avoid the landlord. Short of groceries, I became a patron of a nearby hamburger joint who featured twenty nine cent burgers one day a week. I would buy a couple dozen, keep them in the freezer and live off of them all week.

Fortunately the manager at the Olive Tree apartments was a decent person and took pity on me. One day he caught up with me out in the parking lot. The olive trees which the apartment complex was named after were nice, however they created a nuisance. Olives were constantly falling from the trees and cluttering up and staining the sidewalks and deck. The landlord told me he'd cut my rent in half if I swept the olives up every day. I took him up on his offer, which bought me some time for the rent. However I was still struggling to pay my bills, which included a loan on my brand new Japanese pick-up truck. The landlord, a regular at the Palomino, recommended I go see the manager at the night club. The manager at the Palomino offered me a job sweeping up several nights a week. In addition to the wage he offered, he threw in a meal once a day. I was very grateful when he allowed me the daily meal before I even picked up a broom. I thought it was cool that, while working, I would be listening to top quality entertainment and maybe even rubbing elbows with some of the stars.

Just after the opportunity at The Palomino turned up I got a call from my employer. The building had been repaired and passed inspection; work would resume the next day. And although this should have been good news, and I could not afford to not return to work I was disappointed. The prospect of adventure at The Palomino had really grabbed me and I was reluctant to have to pass it up.

I thanked the manager at The Palomino who extended the offer in case things didn't work out. I was also in debt to my landlord who gave me an additional couple of weeks of grace before bringing my rent up to date. And although I never swept a floor or heard a guitar string twang as a Palomino employee, I am forever grateful for their kind offer, and have many fond memories of the music which wafted down to all of us at the Olive Tree Apartments.

Section IV

GUEST WRITERS

Some of the blogs on Joe's website have been provided by guest writers. We are grateful for their contribution, they have been a popular addition, enjoyed by many. Some of them are featured here.

We think you will enjoy them also.

Guest Writer

Gary Labanow
My life as a Pilot

Introduction

Gary having a little fun on the flight line, back in the day.

This week's guest writer is Gary Labanow. Gary and I have been friends since high school, in addition to having the shared experience of being United States Air Force Vietnam War veterans. Gary actually convinced me to join the Air Force back in the day.

Can't work all the time!

After his military service ended, Gary eventually became a pilot, with an interesting and rewarding career in that endeavor. Over the years I have enjoyed hearing about Gary's flying experiences, and viewing some of the photos and film from his flying days. (We both also enjoy fishing, and swap a few of those stories now and then) Gary has graciously shared some of his experiences with us.

Please enjoy Gary's story.

My Life As A Pilot

Gary enjoyed flying aircraft of all sizes.

I always had an interest in airplanes. I was 16 when I got a job pumping gas at the local airport and used my pay for flight instructions. When I was 17, I got my private pilot's license and was the youngest pilot in Wisconsin. After high school I attended the University of Wisconsin Kenosha Extension. After a year of partying and not doing much studying I realized I was a bit immature for college, ok a lot immature for college. Nineteen sixty-six was a bad year to not be in college and with Uncle Sam looking my way, I joined the US Air Force. I became an aircraft structural repair specialist and soon found myself in Southeast Asia.

After spending time in the Philippines, Thailand, and of course, Vietnam, I decided I needed to get smarter quickly. After my discharge from Luke AFB, Arizona, I went back to college—first at Phoenix College, then Arizona State University (Go Sun Devils) where I majored in mechanical engineering and continued to get more flight ratings.

After getting my multi engine, instrument, flight instructor and instrument instructor ratings I was hired by Lufthansa, a German airline, as a primary flight instructor. It was a great learning experience but I could never fly for their airline as you needed to be a German citizen. After a few years I left Lufthansa and was hired by Continental Airlines where I started my airline career flying as first officer on an ATR-42, a 50-passenger twin engine turboprop. It was a great flying airplane, fun to fly and after a couple years I upgraded to captain.

About this time airlines were moving from turboprop aircraft to all jets. I became captain on an Embraer-145, a 50-passenger jet. My dreams of becoming a jet pilot were finally realized. After a couple years, I transitioned to the Boeing 737. My routes on the 737 covered the US, Canada, Mexico, Central and South America and the Caribbean Islands. I flew the 737 until my retirement at the mandatory age of 60. As fate would have it, about 8 months later they raised the retirement age to 65. So here I was staying home and enjoying retirement when one day my wife said, "I wish you still flew for Continental." I innocently asked why to which she replied, "Because you're home all the time." She had gotten used to having alone time when I was gone 3 or 4 days at a stretch. I took the hint and at 60 years of age, I began looking for a job. I wondered what I wanted to do when I grew up. I had some experience in construction estimating and in sales. I still loved to fly and wondered if any flying jobs were available.

Embraer 145

737-900

My search brought me to an ad from Arizona Game and Fish for a Wildlife Pilot—whatever that was. They were looking for someone with low level flight and tailwheel aircraft experience. Not exactly my airline resume. The pool of applicants must have been small as I was called for an interview. I managed to not terrify the chief pilot on my check ride and got the Cessna 185 on the ground in one piece and thus began the most interesting and fun flying job imaginable.

*We flew all hours.
(Cessna 185)*

The Life of a Wildlife Pilot

One thing they neglected to tell me when I was hired was, we needed to fly when the animals were most active. This is at first light. In Arizona summers first light is about 5am. Since many times we had to fly an hour and a half to the area we were to survey and we had to preflight the airplane that meant leaving home about 2:30am. This was NOT an airline schedule.

Most flights had one or two observers. These were either biologists or Wildlife Managers. Some states have biologists and Game Wardens. These Game Wardens are strictly law enforcement. Arizona Game Wardens are required to have a degree in biology or closely related field. They also go through a law enforcement academy. Thus, our Wildlife Managers are responsible for game management as well as law enforcement.

Telemetry Flights:

Great bunch to work with.

Telemetry flights are the easiest flights we do. Therefore, new pilots start by flying these flights for a couple months. These flights are done about 1500 feet AGL (Above Ground Level). Telemetry flights use an antenna on the airplane to track animals which have been fitted with a transmitting collar. These collars transmit information showing the movements the animal has made. We can see where these animals have been crossing roads allowing overpasses and underpasses to be constructed. This allows animal movements to continue over or under the roadway thus saving the lives of animals and people. We once lost contact with a black bear. We hadn't heard his collar for 3 years when one day we picked up his signal. We downloaded the info and learned he had traveled 300 miles into New Mexico and back three times. Each time we looked for him he was vacationing in New Mexico. Telemetry can also be used to determine migration patterns and nesting areas showing water and habitat requirements. We have tracked elk, deer, antelope, big horn sheep, mountain lion, bear and wolves as well as condors, eagles and even bats.

Photo from aircraft survey.

Survey Flights

After a few months of telemetry flights without breaking an airplane I was trained in survey flights.

Survey flights are conducted following the terrain about 120' AGL and flown as slow as safe for conditions. This requires constant vigilance looking for wires, towers or tall trees. Surveys are flown over a specific hunt unit in a grid pattern with legs ½ mile apart the length of the hunt unit. The observers would count and classify animals as bull, cow or calf (in the case of elk). Each animal species has specific characteristics when seeing the airplane. Antelope will bunch up then try to out run the plane. They are found in very open fairly, level terrain and line up in a straight line running making them the easiest species to survey. Deer are the hardest as they are in mostly forested areas. Trying to spot them under trees is hard and then turning the plane around and trying to determine exactly where it was to check for additional animals in the group requires a lot of practice. Elk tend to be in large groups, sometimes 150 or more. They are not bothered by the plane but sheer numbers can make counting difficult. In some instances, photos are taken for counts on a computer screen. We also survey javelin, big horn sheep, turkeys and sandhill cranes.

My office, Super Cub.

I swear, we weren't lost!

Law Enforcement Flights

During hunt seasons we will look for hunters who have an animal down. We will then direct a WM (Wildlife Manager) to him where he will verify it was a legal kill. We would also conduct night flights looking for poachers using spot lights. If we saw someone spotting, we would guide ground personnel to them. These people would think no one was within miles of them then suddenly a truck, having moved to within about 50' with lights off would light them up with red and blue flashing lights. At this time the poachers were totally surprised and totally shocked. Not all-night stops are tickets. One night a light was spotted moving along a trail through some trees. After guiding a WM to the location, it was determined the kill had been made just at dusk. After gutting the elk, the hunter had been dragging his elk for hours toward his truck. He said he's been hunting for 30 years and never seen a Game Warden then almost midnight one shows up to help him drag and load his kill into his truck. Definitely a surprise.

Some Other Flying Experiences of Arizona Game and Fish

UFO?

Bill, Chief Pilot for the Arizona Game and Fish, spotted what appeared to be a large tarp flapping in the distance. He flew to check it out and found a parachute about the size of a house attached to a metal disk shaped object about the size of a two-car garage with six legs protruding and large metal pads on the ends. The thing had landed and pitched over onto one edge. Bill circled looking for markings, but there were none. He flew back to his office and called the US Weather bureau asking if they had lost some weather gathering object. They had not, but a few minutes later a call came back asking about what was seen and where it was. Bill asked who was calling and the reply was "The United States Government." He gave them the info and decided first thing in the morning he would fly out and take pictures. The next morning, armed with a camera he got to the spot but all that was left were marks where the pads had indented the ground and where the edge had cut into the earth. Nothing more was ever heard about this.

Don't Get Hung Up!

On one desert deer survey our pilot spotted a buck mule deer hanging by his antlers from tree branches. He apparently jumped up to eat some leaves and got hung up. The pilot knowing the animal couldn't live very long and not knowing how long he was caught the pilot landed on a small clearing about a quarter mile away. Our pilot and observer were able to have one grab his legs and the other climbed the tree, grab his antlers and free the deer that was still able to run off.

He was a cute little fella.

Animal Husbandry, Another Part of the Job

One controversial program we flew was supporting the reintroduction of the Mexican Grey Wolf. This was a project with the US Fish and Wildlife Service. Many ranchers and hunters are not in favor of the reintroduction of this predator. Because of the need to protect against inbreeding wolves from other areas are needed. One of the times I was involved was when two three-day old pups were flown from a zoo in Chicago to Phoenix. I then flew the pups, along with two Fish and Wildlife biologists to a mountain area in Arizona. These biologists then placed the pups in the den of a female who had just had five pups of her own. Since wolves can't count when she returned to her den, she continued to raise all seven pups as her own

Did NOT want to end up in this joint!

One of our pilots was asked to fly an injured bald eagle to the vet in Phoenix from Springerville about an hour and a half flight. Normally injured birds and animals are transported in dog kennels so the pilot was a bit surprised when they showed up with the eagle in a cardboard box with the top folded shut. The box was loaded in the back seat and off they went. About 20 minutes into the flight there was noise coming from the back. The pilot looked back and the entire box

Border Patrol, just part of the j.o.b.

was bouncing up and down and white feathers were sticking out of the top. Not wanting to be flying and fighting with an angry eagle he put the plane on autopilot, climbed in back, pushed the eagle's head down, tied the box securely with the seat belt, climbed back up front and continued another "normal day" in the life of a Wildlife Pilot.

Locked Up Abroad?

Every two years we would conduct a week long survey in Mexico in conjunction with Mexican biologists to study the Sonoran Pronghorn, an endangered species found in southern Arizona and northern Mexico. We normally flew three single engine survey planes and a twin engine filled with spare parts should a problem develop with any of the planes. One year with the twin down for maintenance we loaded a truck with parts and our mechanic drove to meet us in Mexico. All went well right up to reaching Mexico Customs where he was detained for smuggling parts for sale in Mexico. After being held at the border for 8 hours, almost ending up in a Mexican prison, and numerous phone calls to the Mexican Consulate, he was allowed to continue. That was the last time we used a truck to bring parts to Mexico.

I did however on another trip to Mexico breeze completely innocent through customs and upon emptying my suitcase in my room discovered a full box of .30-06 ammo in a side pocket. Those shells are now somewhere far out in the Mexican desert.

Add Border Patrol to Our Resume

We often see illegal immigrants in the desert. The Arizona desert is deadly in the summer with temperatures reaching over 120 degrees. One time a group of immigrants were spotted laying down with a few waving at the plane. Border patrol was called and guided to the group. Several were within hours of death. Our pilot received a lifesaving award. Unfortunately, we are not always in time. On one survey flight our pilot spotted a body. It turned out he had been dead for a couple days. The Arizona desert can be both beautiful and deadly.

A Fine End To An Interesting Career

My last flight before retiring from Game and Fish was an antelope survey. On our last leg we flew over two buck antelope that had been fighting, one on each side of a barb wire fence. They both were tangled in the fence and couldn't have lived very long tangled. The WM with me called the ranch owner on his cell phone. He was able to drive out to the spot, cut one strand, and free both animals. A nice end to a wonderful career.

A beautiful animal, antelope occasionally die when fighting males lock horns.

Guest Writer

RICK WEHLER NORWEGIAN STYLE TURKEY BINGO

INTRODUCTION

Rick, in full cow bell regalia

Rick Wehler is a humorist and a published author. Many of Rick's stories are posted on his Facebook page. His books are a compilation of stories in which Rick relates some of his life experiences, through a slightly twisted but humorous slant.

Rick has shared some of his stories with me, so I can share them with others. An adventurous outing at a bingo game with his wife Cora, is the subject of this article. I believe you will enjoy Rick's Bingo game adventure.

Part4 : Guest Writers

OUR BINGO ADVENTURE

My wife, Cora, and I had chosen the weekend before Thanksgiving to visit her Ma, her brother Richie and his fiancée Debby in their Northern Minnesota hometown, population 1,000, rife with Norwegians.

Upon our arrival, Ma informed us of the family events for that evening: a heart-healthy meal of the best broasted chicken around, lovingly prepared by the gourmet chefs at The Deer Creek Feed and Bleed, followed by the V.F.W. Turkey Bingo Fundraiser.

After gobbling all the fowl we could stuff, our group proceeded to the Community Center in time for the gaming. Even though my poor luck at gambling had become family folklore, I did not wish to earn an additional rep as party pooper and agreed to attend the function.

The building's interior was crammed wall-to-wall with lunchroom-type tables, a myriad of clanking metal folding chairs and hundreds of local residents. I couldn't help but wonder who was milking the cows. Due to the overflow turn-out, several sought-after chairs up front uncomfortably accommodated more than one backside each.

At an entrance table Ma purchased the use of one well-used bingo card for each of us, although some of the patrons purchased as many as five cards.

We found an unoccupied table with no chairs by the back door. Upon our request, one of the V.F.W. regulars recruited five chairs, which he found hidden out back in the shed. He tramped our way in his jingling, unbuckled rubber boots, fur hat with ear flaps and dangling straps, foggy glasses, well-worn, wet work gloves and an open jacket. He leaned the frost-covered metal folding chairs against our table and accepted our thanks.

All of the event's officials were located way up in front: Hilde, the bingo machine operator, dressed in a flowered blouse with a flamboyant breast pin, Einar, the announcer, bedecked in his V.F.W. hat bedizened with multiple awards, and Olga, the game's judge, who sported transparent nasal air tubes, which led into an oxygen tank hidden under the table.

I learned from Einar's announcement that I was to endure 15 bingo games that evening. Previous to this, I was willingly ignorant of the many different bingo versions—regular bingo, 4-corners bingo, X-bingo, picture frame bingo and black-out bingo. I felt certain that my fabled ill-fortune would continue.

Games 1 through 4 passed uneventfully. All winners were somewhere within Olga's hearing. Several losers traded in their unlucky cards in hopes of finding one with inherent good fortune. I felt no need to trade my card and reduce my meager chances to zero, like the temperature of my hinder.

Game 5 produced a winner at our table as Richie yelled, "Bingo." The rules required the judge to authenticate his winning numbers. Mr. Jingling Boot Buckles was kind enough to act on Olga's behalf. Yup, Richie's victory was confirmed. Mr. Ear Flaps opened the back door, retrieved Richie's prize from the bed of a pickup truck and dropped an 11 lb. turkey on our table with an ice cracking thud. We sensed the envious stares from the multiple-card-holding occupants of adjacent tables.

Game 7, a four-corner game in which the winner must–oh just figure it out–was won by Ma. (None of my four corners participated.) Mr. Foggy Glasses repeated the verification and turkey presentation. Our frozen table guest, the turkey, now had a mate. I didn't fret about hanky-panky on their part. I believe that frozen turkeys are neutered. We again bore the gaze of jealous rivals.

As Game 8 commenced, I finally found employment for a few of my game tokens upon the bingo card. What, four in a row? Why that's almost a winner!

I stared at the column's remaining uncovered position, O-69. I concentrated on the cipher. I moved my lips and spoke it silently, attempting to hypnotize Einar from afar. As I once again mouthed 0-69, I did so in unison with Einar. Wha, wha, what? I, I, won. "Bingo!" Oh yes, Olga heard me alright. A legion of tonight's neglected cows in a hundred abandoned barns mooed in praise of my accomplishment.

Mr. Well-Worn, Wet Work Gloves once again verified the triumphant numbers and plunked another turkey onto our table. In geometry three points determine a plane. In this bingo hall, three turkeys nearly fomented a riot.

The mood settled a bit as game 9 began. I followed along, even though I was shivering from my chilly chair, the continued icy wind blasts from the back door, the fog radiating from the thawing turkeys, the competitor's cold stares and my recent good luck. OMG, I filled another full line! Dare I, should I, oh why not? Freaking "BINGO!" I have no doubt that several people at nearby tables soiled themselves. I am fairly sure that I did. Mr. Open Jacket followed his proven procedure with a little extra thunk. We then owned 43 pounds of frozen fowl.

The following game, a blackout—cover all the numbers—was won elsewhere as were games 11 and 12. Game 13, however, was a game that will live in the annals of V.F.W. Turkey Bingo history, as Cora screamed, "Bingo!" Never before had one small group of contestants won so many games.

By now our team was on a first-name basis with our V.F.W. assistant, Jingles, his preferred moniker. He leaned against the building's back wall with his arms and boots crossed and smiled as he watched the melt water drip from our 54 pound prodigious poultry pile while the final two games were won by other contenders.

We left our lucky bingo cards on the table as Jingles enabled our escape through the back door with our five thawing turkeys and five frozen fannies.

Rick's books may be purchased on Amazon.

Guest Writer

George C. Dooley WWII Diary

Introduction

World War II was the largest military engagement in the history of man. Some sixty million people or three percent of the world population perished in the calamity, with many more millions wounded and maimed. During that time, sixteen million U.S. citizens served in the armed forces, of which over four hundred and fifty thousand were killed and some six hundred thousand wounded. Many millions of U.S. citizens also served on the home front, aiding the war effort in various ways.

Sprouting from the unfinished business of earlier wars, the Axis powers of Germany, Italy, Japan and their allies, fell into totalitarianism manifested by tyranny, nationalism, aggression and genocide. Great Britain, the United States, the Soviet Union, France, China and their allies opposed the Axis powers. The war began in 1939 and ended with the fall of Germany and Japan in 1945. Many trillions of dollars were consumed fueling the war, and when it was finally over many nations lay in ruins.

Many of us today are connected to the war through our fathers, mothers, grandfathers, aunts, uncles and other relatives who served in the war or kept the home fires burning. We are fortunate to have heard and read about many of their personal stories during that time.

George C Dooley

Today's guest writer is George C. Dooley. Mr. Dooley served in the U.S. Navy from 1942 to 1946. Dooley served on the U.S.S. Ruby, a civilian yacht that was converted into a minesweeper. Although he passed away in 1995, we are fortunate that Mr. Dooley kept a diary of his service during that time and it has been made available to us. Like many who served during times of war, Mr. Dooley's memoir reflects periods of boredom, excitement, fear and hope.

GEORGE S DOOLEY

I became friends with Mr. Dooley's son, George S. Dooley, while we were both living in Southern California in the early 1970s. George S. Dooley is a United States Air Force Vietnam Era Veteran. George and his wife Diane live in the state of Washington near his son and grandson. I am grateful to George for making his Dad's diary available to us.

George S. Dooley

Please enjoy George C. Dooley's World War II diary, in his words:

U.S.S. RUBY

On the 10th of April 1945 we left Key West, Fla. for Panama City and through the canal where we arrived at 7:30 April 20, 1945. After spending a day there we left on the 22nd for Pearl Harbor. After a 16 day trip we arrived at Pearl Harbor on the 16th of May. After spending a two week stay there and having a grand time we pulled out June 8th for Enewetak. After 3 days of travelling we arrived there safe and sound also on the 12th of June. We stayed there for two weeks and then pulled out for Guam. We arrived there on the 25th of June in which I met an old buddy Chris Fields. I surely had a grand time there and then after a swell time we left then on the 8th of July for Okinawa. Since we arrived here, we had two alerts and so far no action.

George C. Dooley

On the 8th of August I witnessed my first air attack and bombing in which the plane dropped his bombs and then in a few seconds crashed only a few yards away from us which sent up a large cloud of smoke and flames. Since this at-

 tack they have been coming over every night.

Well on the 10th of August I seen some of the largest gun fire after the Japs had announced they were willing to surrender and we accepted.

Sunday morning August 11th 1945 we were waiting patiently for the word of surrender and at 0900 no word as yet.

While at anchorage at Naha Bay, we had one of the closest calls ever to see while on our way for fuel. We came within ten feet of being blown up because of Japanese floating mine but of course luck was again with us and after a few hours, a minesweeper picked it up.

On the 14th of August at 2:15 while listening to the radio and important broadcast came over that the Japanese had offered to surrender and on the 16th we had received word that the war was over. This was one of the happiest moments of my life. On the 16th of August we had orders to go on the ping line until further notice. While on the ping line we were ordered back to Hell's Anchorage to take a supply and oil and to stand by.

On the morning of the 30th we had orders to report with the greatest force of mine sweepers ever assembled out here and then we pulled out for our destination which was between the Yellow Sea and thru the strait to the Sea of Japan. On the 1st of September we arrived at our destination and so far good luck is with us. After this sweep was over we were ordered to move over to Nagasaki and on this sweep we had gotten six mines to our credit.

On the morning of Sept. 18th 1945 we pulled into the naval base of Sasebo which of course is one of Japan's greatest. There were quite a few Jap ships but none of any value to them. They were either hit by our ships or beached to save them. This place is located just north of Nagasaki and we were one of the first ships to arrive here and also at Korea and Nagasaki. Today we are waiting for a typhoon to pass over. After a two day stay there and of course safe we heard that one of the mine sweepers had capsized and only one man was found. On the morning of the 20th we came back to Natura Shim and stayed there until Sunday morning which of course was the 22nd of Sept. About 0530 we were under way this time to go straight into Nagasaki and I witnessed the mass landing of occupational troops to land here and also seen where the first atomic bomb was dropped. It sure did a great deal of damage and after a few hours there we came back to Anchorage.

From the 23rd of Sept. until the 1st of October we have been carrying mail to Natusu Shina and to Sacebo Hanbar and back. So far there has been quite and a few rumors that we will be on our way back to the States before Christmas, but as of yet no word. All this week we had boiler trouble and as of yet has not been fixed.

Well today October 3, 1945 we were given liberty in Sasebo, Japan and the town what was left of it was pretty good and the Japs treated us good and the little children were always begging us for cigarettes and in exchange gave us Jap money. I really had a swell time and it was the first liberty in six months. The place was very dirty and it was a complete loss to the Japs. All their main buildings were completely destroyed by our bombs and only a few remained. I got some souvenirs and also some Jap money and spent a swell day looking around.

Since the third until the 26th of October we have been in Sasebo and getting liberty every other day. I went on a souvenir party and now have a Jap rifle and bayonet.

On the 26th we went on another mine sweeping job which ought to take around fourteen days.

Today October 29th we went out and we now have seven more mines to our credit. We are now anchored in the Yellow Sea just north of Okinawa. We came back from this sweep safe and sound and since this time we have been anchored in Sasebo harbor.

On the 18th of November we received word that this ship would return at last on the 20th of November for the states. Everyone is excited and some men are going to be transferred. I have my fingers crossed that I will stay aboard to bring it back.

Nov. 19th 1945 we are to take on supplies this date.

The ship has three stops before reaching the states

Eniwetok, Pearl Harbor and then on to San Diego.

With luck I expect to be on it. Well today I was the happiest fellow in the Navy because on this date the 20th of Nov. at 4:30 we set out for the states and it was a wonderful sight to see our homeward bound pennant flying. I waited a long time for this day and was very happy to leave Japan because I had seen enough of it. Our first stop on the way back to the states is Eniwetok and then on to Pearl Harbor. We are scheduled to arrive there on the 5th of Dec. but it may take longer.

We arrived at Eniwetok on the 29th of Nov. at 0830 and left there on the 30th. So far from Eniwetok we had swell weather. We are now scheduled to arrive at Pearl Harbor on the 9th of December. After a short stay we pulled out of Pearl Harbor for San Diego, CA. We arrived there on the 21st of Dec. at 0900. While there I had a swell time and also had the chance to go across the border into Mexico. I really enjoyed myself in San Diego and also Hollywood, Calif. We left San Diego on the 30th of January now heading for Key West, Fla. Tonight on the fourth of Feb. just four days away from Panama. We arrived at Panama on the 9th of Feb. Spent a good time there and left Panama on the 12th of Feb. for Key West, Fla. Had a swell trip and pulled into Key on the 18th of Feb.

Today Feb. 28th 1946, I just have 15 more days left before leaving the ship. On the 14th of March I left the ship to go to the receiving ship which is located in Key West. I arrived there at 10:00 and spent seven days there and on the night of the 21st we left Key West by bus for Miami, Fla to catch the 8:10 train for New York.

We arrived on the twenty second in New York and got on the train for Boston and arrived at the Largo building at 7:00 clock and three days later was a civilian once again.

This ended my Navy career after 3 and a half years.

***

Thank you Mr. Dooley, God bless you and all of our Veterans and may God Bless America!

Guest Writer

STEVE TINDALL BEING TALL

INTRODUCTION

Rich, Joe and Steve at a recent event featuring veterans who write.

My friend Steve Tindall is a U.S. Navy veteran, and a fellow author. In addition to being very active with Veteran's causes and events, Steve writes about his experiences during his naval career. At six foot, five inches tall, Steve bumped up against some unique challenges on board ship. (A problem I never had, I assure you)

Steve has shared one of his humorous stories with us. I believe you will get a chuckle out of "Being Tall."

Part 4: Guest Writers

BEING TALL

I've been encouraged by my friend and fellow veteran author Joe Campolo Jr. to write more about the time I spent in the Navy to augment my book. And so, here is more information about the interesting things my height introduced into my time in service.

In my book I talk about some of the issues surrounding being somewhat oversized for destroyers. I was 6' 5" tall with BIG feet so things which were normal for most people ended up being a challenge for me. But not all of my challenges were aboard ship.

During "C" school on the Mark 37 Gun Fire Control System we were inspected every morning of class. One of my instructors was a very short (by anyone's

standards, not just mine!) Chief Petty Officer. I had just purchased a new "Dixie Cup" style hat and had stored it overnight with the edges rolled up to give it the right look. (See picture above)

Or so I thought. While it had the right curved over appearance top to bottom it looked more like a box someone sat on from side to side. It had four distinct corners to it which were NOT equally distant from each other. On my head I couldn't tell how bad it looked but the Chief sure could.

Steve next to his berth

I'm standing at attention which means you look straight ahead and don't move your head around at all. So, when the Chief gets to me, I can't see him at all. I just hear this "Where did you get that hat?" coming from somewhere. I didn't

Part4 : Guest Writers

move so I hear the same line issued again, a little bit more forcefully this time. I still didn't move so the third time it came out much louder: "Where did you get that #^#$%^# hat!" I chanced a look to my left, then to my right, and then straight down where I discovered a very angry man staring up at me. My having to look down on him didn't help his mood. I explained briefly my hat was new which didn't mollify him at all and he proceeded to explain to me in VERY colorful language my hat was a disgrace and if caught in one like that again I would be sent to the fleet as a professional deck swabber and not a Fire Control Technician! The next day my hat was squared away and no further comments were necessary.

Steve today, "How did I ever squeeze into those things?"

I managed to complete "C" school successfully and reported to my first ship. After I checked in, I was escorted down to our berthing compartment to unpack. Several of my new fellow FTs gathered around to find out more about the new guy. It was when I pulled out my boon dockers (steel toed half boots) the space suddenly got quiet. I thought I had done something wrong when one of them said: "I see you brought the new life boats with you!" We all had a good laugh and passed around our new vessels and I was frequently reminded of the incident during my time aboard to another round of laughter.

Steve Tindall was born in the small town of Amboy, NY, just a little West of Syracuse. After graduating from high school, he joined the U.S. Navy, where he learned electronics, security, and how to make his bed properly.

He served on two destroyers and spent the final two years of his nine-year enlistment instructing at the Naval Training Center, Great Lakes, IL. He transitioned to the data networking field, specializing in capacity analysis and protocol interpretation. He wrote several work-related articles for various publications including a two-year stint as the editor of a satirical monthly newsletter designed to improve morale at work. He retired on April Fool's Day in 2016 and spends his time improving veterans lives and educating the public about our military history.

Steve's old vessel

Steve's book "Underway!" can be purchased on Amazon.

https://www.amazon.com/Underway-sailors-story-aboard-destroyers-ebook/dp/B07X42VWJ6/ref=sr_1_2?dchild=1&keywords=underway+steve+tindall&qid=1585218891&sr=8-2

Guest Writer

DICK EVENSON LEADERSHIP

Today's guest writer is Dick Evenson. Dick, a friend of mine for many years, founded and manages TWS Consulting; a highly successful marketing company. Dick is semi-retired and lives in Northern Illinois with his wife Georgia. Dick and Georgia enjoy spending time with their children and grandchildren. Dick has shared his thoughts on Leadership. Thanks for visiting my website.

Joe

LEADERSHIP!

Dick and Georgia Evenson

I start each day by opening lines of communication with the outside world. My choices are USA Today online for national/international news, The Chicago Tribune online for the latest crime report and the Lake County News Sun for current information on my neighbors. Throw in a daily perusal of Facebook for pictures of people's grandchildren (including mine) and you can establish a pretty solid basis for becoming the know-it-all you've always wanted to be.

As I told my wife when I semi-retired, count on me to do three things: read, write and rest. So I have a constant supply of books I'm reading simultaneously.

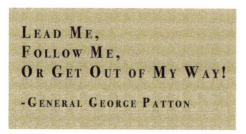

For the Leadership Question, two have been helpful: *The Art of Leadership*, a zippy little dissertation on what leaders should and shouldn't do; plus Bill O'Reilly's book, *Old School* which introduces the concept that the modern world is divided into two groups: Old School and Snowflakes.

The Art of Leadership is written in a total of 111 pages by J. Donald Walters, a British publisher who died in 2013 at the age of 87. This is the type of book you find at the checkout station of your Barnes & Noble bookstore and can't resist buying. I whizzed through the book in two hours and here's what I learned:

— Leadership is not an ego game

— Leadership means taking responsibility and setting aside personal desires

— Leadership means service, loyalty and support

— Leadership means taking action, not relying only on talk

— Leadership is intuition guided by common sense

— Leadership is an art

I agree with all of Mr. Walters conclusions. His views on leadership might seem to be slightly dated, but his major points are spot-on to me. Especially the part about the taking responsibility for your people above all.

Old School is not specifically about leadership. Instead it's a clever book about growing up in a time past when values, integrity and discipline were the cornerstones of civilized behavior. Mr. O'Reilly, currently being run out of Fox News, claims that today's younger workers and their "leaders" have degenerated into a misguided, crusading cult of Snowflakes. These are people who wake up whining about safe spaces, being marginalized by their college's mascots, practicing diversification and deciding what to protest each day. I agree with the author that these folks tend to be pains-in-the-ass whether they are trying to "lead" or being led.

So What Is Wrong With Today's Leaders?

First of all, let's get one thing straight. Management is not leadership. Management is manipulating people to get them to do what you want, like meeting a sales forecast or achieving a profit level. People, whether they are Old School or Snowflakes, can see right through that crap. They know that these kind of "leaders" don't give a rat's behind about their work lives and career goals. So they put up with the single-minded purpose of the manager until they get fed up. Then they leave, in many cases for jobs that their previous employer can't fathom.

Granted, today's employee (a majority of whom are Snowflakes) can be a challenge for even a true leader. They job-hop at a moment's notice. They want to be recognized and praised on a minute-by-minute basis. They have firm opinions on everything and want to be heard all the time. And more than likely, they upset Old Schoolers just by being around the office.

That being said, the lack of leadership today still falls on the people in charge. In a nutshell, too many of them are not focused on building a team that meets the goals of everyone. Often, they have no knowledge of their employees including names, job functions, family and career aspirations. These executives are Manipulators and they use people to advance their own causes and enhance their bank accounts. When they no longer need you, you're gone, often right before the holidays.

These Manipulators often use clever writers to convey messages that any employee can and does see through. I've been fortunate in my career to only have applied my ghostwriting skills to company executives who are true leaders.

Here are three examples of real leaders I have experienced:

Terry Ruhlman.

Terry was brought into The Ansul Company in Marinette, WI, in the wake of a less-than-perfect takeover by a foreigner who looked and acted more like the clown in North Korea than a corporate leader. Anyway, Terry kicked out the infidels and began rebuilding Ansul into the fine company it had once been and would be again. We were all a little fat and lazy so Terry had a habit of calling his managers at 7:00 a.m. to ask a random question. We soon figured out that 7:00 a.m. was the starting time, not 8:00 a.m. or 9:00. From there, he built us back into a single team with the right focus and the discipline to achieve our goals.

Brad Sebstad.

Brad was my partner in the Chicago-based agency of Sebstad, Lutrey & Evenson. He was a clever writer, corporate strategist and raconteur who told some of the best stories about the advertising business. His philosophy was simple: respect your employees, always treat your clients right and screw the government anytime you can. Brad also coined the phrase, "Never own a business where you must maintain a public bathroom." That just about says it all.

Mickey Reiss.

Mickey has spent his entire career running companies. When he came into Rolf Jensen & Associates, he was replacing a legend, Rolf Jensen. What most people didn't understand was that Mickey was a Leader while Rolf was a Manipulator. Mickey faced a very talented but arrogant group of technical people who needed discipline. He began by instituting his personal belief... Always Do the Right Thing. For your clients, for your profession, for your colleagues and for yourself. Somehow, you always knew that Mickey was aggressive but wanted the best for each one of us.

So what's the bottom line on Leadership?

It all boils down to three things. Here's what I'd tell anyone who wanted to know how to be a more effective leader:

1. Terry was right. Before you can lead a group of people, you need to get their attention and explain where the team is going and why. It helps if you also know each and every one of them.

2. Brad was right. You need to respect your employees, but revere your clients.

3. Mickey was right. Do the right thing. Always.

Guest Writer

Penni Evans
Frozen in Bronze

This week's guest writer is Penni Evans. Penni began writing poetry and short essays at the age of fifteen. Encouraged by her grandmother, Amah, herself a writer, Penni dreamed of far-away places and world travel.

After she earned a Bachelor's degree in political science, Penni volunteered for duty with the Red Cross organization. Through them, Penni became a Donut Dollie and was sent to Vietnam.

Slogging through the mud, life in Nam.

Vietnam took its toll on Penni as it did with many who served there. After her tour, she spent six months back packing across Europe. She worked for other non-profit organizations and obtained a Masters degree in Human

Behavior.

At a Red Cross reunion in San Francisco in 1983, Penni's emotional healings from the Vietnam War began. She started writing poetry which has been published in various Women's and Veteran's venues. She also has been active in many Women Veteran's issues. Penni currently lives in Colorado with three very close feline friends.

Penni has graciously shared her poetry with me, to share with all. The following is a poem she penned after the Vietnam Women's Memorial in Washington D.C., which she had a part in creating, was dedicated in 1993. I believe you will enjoy "Frozen in Bronze."

FROZEN IN BRONZE

Who are you, my sister
I look into your eyes and see my soul
You are frozen in bronze, forever young
What are your memories, your thoughts
What words have been spoken
For your ears only
The secrets you hold in your heart
Are mine also

Will your voice ever be heard
Can the words locked so deep within
Ever be free to drift on the wind
Can the night of the endless dark

Ever become the dawn of a new day
Will we as sisters ever heal
From wounds suffered
In silence a lifetime ago

We were healers
Warriors and angels of truth
No matter what clothes we wore
Nor where we worked
Nor the time we served
Our duties may have been varied
But my sister
We were all together

We can come visit you
And in so doing
We can visit
The self we left behind
So many years
So many tears
So many memories ago.

Section V

Philosophy

All writers have a philosophical nature, and Joe certainly fits that category. In this section, we feature some of Joe's philosophy, along with the philosophy of others, who Joe has selected.

Philosophical Quips & Quotes from Joe

You are welcome to share Joe's quotes, please credit him as the author if you do. Thank you

On the high seas!

The Internet is a great source of information. For example, I've learned that all the climatologists among us are also epidemiologists, legal scholars and political affairs experts.

Give them something to love, something to hate or both.

Part 5: Philosophy

Upon being surprised by a predator in the wild, your memory is seared for eternity.

If you never jump the fence, you will only understand your half of the pasture

Why take the high road, the low road is easier and you'll have some esteemed company.

In war, everybody loses. Participants sacrifice their lives, limbs and sanity, perpetrators their morality.

I dislike all of these exposes, investigative reports and heavily researched articles on our heroes from the past.

We are learning they were, on occasion, ignorant, insensitive and even flawed... just like us

Part 5: Philosophy

Nobody thinks it can happen here....until it happens here.

Most of the real monsters in history started out as bullies. They became monsters when they found out they could get away with being bullies.

Someone noted that I'm a bit of a cynic, whereby I noted that, yes, I am quite sane.

Are we virtuous because it's the right thing to do...or is it fear of divine punishment that guides our moral compass?

I've enjoyed many things in life, I've celebrated much, I've witnessed a great deal, I've had a full share.

Yet on a beautiful day, with the sun in the sky, the clouds billowing high, a gentle breeze passing by, I dream of catching just one more fish, taking another warm swim, watching the sun set once more, and seeing another smile on the face of my grandchildren.

Part 5: Philosophy

The people of China and Russia are subdued, as a result of centuries of servitude, war and other tragedies. Americans ... Americans are new at it, they complain and resist. May they be forever young.

The person who lies to themself may be the worst liar of them all. For both the liar and the person being lied to, are aware of the truth.

I was never smart enough to be a crook or a politician. Forgive me if I've repeated myself.

Insomnia may be the worst affliction of them all. Up and down, throughout the night, you face your demons over and over. You maintain a watchful eye on the window, waiting for the dawn to dissipate your torments.

You can give the bear your apple, but he's still gonna want your sandwich.

Part 5: Philosophy

When people hear I volunteered to go to Vietnam, they mistakenly believe I was brave. As I soon discovered, I was stupid.

The mosaic of our life starts before we are even born, with some pieces already in place, hard wired genetically. Parents, guardians, teachers and mentors plant others as we grow. Upon adulthood we assume full responsibility for our mosaic and place, plant and move pieces as we travel along through the web of life. By the time our end is near, the mosaic is almost complete, a design unique to each individual who has ever occupied our planet. And though we will pass, the mosaic of our life will influence others, who are left to complete their own mosaic, as they travel along on life's journey.

Always overstate the strength of your enemy, if you win you will be a hero, if you lose, a martyr.

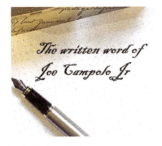

My mind is always writing. At times, I get it on paper.

Though the child is bitten by a mosquito, the parent feels the sting of a bee.

Drawing by Catherine Ryan

Staring into the abyss, holds little trepidation for those who live there

Truth is no longer the fulcrum of our existence. We determine what we wish to believe, move into that camp and defend it at all costs.

You can tell how powerful someone is by the amount of hate they generate.

Little Greta Thunberg, climate change activist

Part 5: Philosophy

The scent of a skunk is most readily detected by another skunk.

Discard your age, your station, or any other limits you may have assigned yourself…do what you wish without preconditions…and you will be fulfilled.

In each of us there lies a hero, and in each of us there lies a coward. Which ever one we see depends upon a myriad of circumstance.

In Vietnam, you could really "let out the badger."

Getting him back in was the trick.

One only need glance at Dante's Inferno to glimpse what a disease, such as malaria, can do.

(Dante suffered with it most of his life)

Part 5: Philosophy

We are each given an infinitesimal chance at the universe. What will we do with that chance?

Our anger often surpasses the level of our intelligence.

Crime and punishment is a real dilemma for our "civilized society." Just what to do with those real bad guys?

People can change...people can also change back.

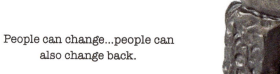

Part 5: Philosophy

If the ignorance of some people could be
harnessed as an energy source,
the sun would pale in comparison.

Fear of humiliation is the only thing
standing between man
and total bedlam.

Maimed for the value of it's horn

If man is the most intelligent species, he
has yet to prove it.

Part 5: Philosophy

Good teachers impart knowledge,
great teachers inspire us to seek knowledge.

My best friend Jim, (RIP) and his wife Tess. Both excellent educators.

Is it I that you
fear, or that
which I've
stirred in your
head?

Part 5: Philosophy

To those among us who reject science and rail at folks in that endeavor, just remember it was the scientist who developed the process to extract the energy you consume in your trailer, and it was the scientist who mastered the art of metallurgy used throughout your pick-up truck, and it was the scientist who developed the process to preserve all that food at the Golden Corral.

Those who desperately seek power, are the bane of mankind.

If you find yourself engulfed in darkness, you learn Braille.

My ability to tolerate fools seems to have diminished along with my hearing.

Part 5: Philosophy

When it comes to money, trust no one but your dog... and then sleep with one eye open.

If I've not reacted to any offense of note..... don't let your guard down just yet.

I don't believe I've ever regretted any acts of kindness I may have committed. No doubt could have and should have done a few more.

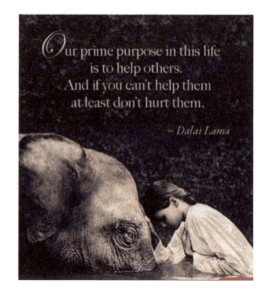

Part 5: Philosophy

The best years of our lives come and go without our even realizing it. At the time, we think those days will never end, they slip away little by little, and we hardly take notice. When reality sets in and we realize those days will not return, the disappointment is stunning and almost unbearable.

VA health care is like Forest Gump's box of chocolates, you never know what you're gonna get.

In some instances deafness is an advantage, blindness is a blessing, and death is a mercy.

Part 5: Philosophy

If it was easy, everyone would do it.

(I got this one)

I get now, why old folks are sometimes cranky. They are aware there is much left to be done....though there's probably not enough sand left in the glass.

Weak minded people gravitate towards despots, like moths to a flame.

Dishonesty in discord is a form of surrender.

Part 5: Philosophy

Some of my best stories will not appear on my blog.

If you don't share this you're a heartless servant of the devil!

Like many others today I use and follow Facebook. I use it to follow the activities of family and friends, and also to promote my writing. When I first joined FB several years ago, it was dominated by young people posting about their dating and sporting activities. After us "geezers" discovered FB it soon became festooned with recipe exchanges and medical issues.

The past two or three years has seen FB become politically polarized. It seems that many people on both sides of the spectrum feel that their political beliefs are the only ones of any value and this belief allows them to plaster my FB page with copy and paste memes, political insults, and in many cases "fake news".

I don't really mind someone posting their political point of view if it is original, well thought out and vetted for facts. But I very much mind the many that are none of the above. I find the whole thing irritating and discouraging; as I'm sure many others do.

If you read and follow this blog, please keep in mind that while some forums are appropriate for political ranting, others are not. DON'T KILL FACEBOOK WITH POLITICAL RANTS, hey?!

Part 5: Philosophy

I don't need a big chunk of money to make me happy ... a medium chunk would do.

I've always enjoyed listening to the Dalai Lama, Mr. Rogers, Dr. Phil and people like that. I admire their gentle and accepting nature. I often think...Now why can't I be like that? But alas...I cannot...I'll keep working at it though.

After every tragedy we are implored to get religion into our lives—then scolded for worshiping false Gods. I wish they would make up their minds.

Through our parents we look behind us, through our children we look ahead.

Part 5: Philosophy

The painter gives it vision, the musician gives it voice, the writer gives it meaning.

Back in the early days of science fiction, humans in the 21st century were depicted as being immensely intelligent, tolerant and peace loving.

I believe a new timetable is in order.

Based upon every living creature we know of past or present, (especially humans) any aliens who decide to visit our planet, probably aren't coming to enjoy the holidays with us.

Like blowing sand in the desert, our experiences gather in ever growing hills cast over our lifetime.

PTSD and Agent Orange are the uninvited guests that followed us home.

Part 5: Philosophy

Being a Writer is like being a Farmer. You keep at it till the money's all gone.

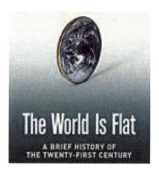

Sharing a popular opinion may bring us satisfaction, however it may not always bring us truth.

You can learn quite a bit about a person by observing how they treat people they don't have to be nice to.

There is no stronger advocate for Democracy than a nation that has been under Communist, Fascist, Nazi or Monarch rule for any length of time. However that democracy must be nurtured, protected, watched over and scrutinized...lest the scoundrels have their way.

Part 5: Philosophy

They were driven off of their land and laid waste with pestilence; after which they were taught religion...so they could save themselves.

If you walked a mile in these, you would have seen enough...

My Mom was great. She always had my back. She was a voracious reader and encouraged me to write. In my mind, she's still looking over my shoulder covering me. Moms do that, even when they are gone.

I used to be a young man but forsook my youth for age and wisdom...thus far I have succeeded in getting old.

I speak through the river, I see through the sky, I hear through the wind.

The American mid-west has some of the most fertile farmland in the world. It is being paved over with concrete and asphalt at an alarming rate. Giant warehouses are popping up like mushrooms along every interstate. Ironically, these giant warehouses are used to store products imported from third world countries; who import farm goods from the U.S.

Metaphorically speaking, I'm not going to get into the ring with Hemingway.

My greatest fear is that we have yet to see the worst of man.

Part 5: Philosophy

U.S. Marine stands with Vietnamese children as they watch their house burn after an Allied patrol set it ablaze after finding communist AK-47 ammunition, Jan. 13, 1971. Patrol made up of U.S. Marines and South Vietnamese popular forces searched the village, 25 miles south of Da Nang. (AP Photo)

Joe's note: Winning the hearts and minds? In my opinion this practice was one reason the war went bad. I never understood the logic behind this type of activity.

The end of one war sows the seeds of another.

I've always been appreciative of where I've been, though I may have no wish to repeat the visit.

What's in a Name? Joe's take on Shakespeare's Comment

You are welcome to share Joe's quotes, please credit him as the author when you do.

Willy

Areas called "No Man's Land" are usually so called due to the activity of man.

Well...who knew the new gnu?

If it isn't a Budweiser, it must be a ...

They called it the "Highway of Death" for good reason

Wars of Choice.... are seldom fought by those who chose them.

Why you dirty... (fill in the blanks)

Some time ago I railed against a man made environmental disaster that had decimated a popular fishery. For my actions I was labeled a "tree hugger."

More recently I applauded the efforts of a mining company in saving an old growth stand of pines near their operation. On this occasion I was likened to a "robber baron."

Now, I may have hugged a few trees over the years, especially in my youth when I liked to climb them, but the act was only a matter of survival, I assure you. And although I certainly am guilty of having filched my share of office supplies on occasion, I "ain't no Jesse James," as they say.

I kind of like being called a "baron," however I have never actually met one and other than watching the professional wrestler "Baron Von Raschke" mercilessly apply his claw hold on unwitting opponents, I have no experience in the area.

Rock...Paper...Shears?

When I was a kid we had a pair of scissors at home. They were kept in a special drawer and only withdrawn at the approval of my mother, who among other things was the guardian of important stuff. They were much better than the tinny junk scissors we used for school work. Sometimes I would secretly open the drawer and take them out. I liked the solid feel and weight of them.

A $395 pair of "scissors"

Later in junior high school, I noted that some of our teachers referred to scissors as "shears." These shears were treated with even more circumspect than my mother's scissors in the guarded drawer at home. After that, I naturally associated shears with a special degree of importance. "You may get the shears, Joseph." Right on, Teach!

A $395 pair of "shears"

Later, working in industry I noticed that almost all scissors were referred to as "shears." I believe "shear operator" had a certain impact, versus "scissors cutter." Better pay grade perhaps?

A cursory investigation finds that in theory, some define the distinction between scissors and shears by length, though not in practice. And yet many others separate the two by price, but here again a quick investigation reveals some very expensive scissors, along with some very expensive shears.

And another thing, why are they referred to as a pair? You only use one. The whole business is a shear mystery to me.

What about Fido?

Meet "Eugene."

People love their pets. The names of their pets sometimes reflect the pets personality...or the personality the pet owner wishes they had—Sparky, Smoky, Precious, Lucky, for example. Other people use objects to name their pets—Tank, Diesel, to name a few.

And still others apply regal names to their furry friends—King, Duke, Lady, Prince being some of the more popular names of royalty we often find applied to our canine charges. Many dogs are named after other animals. Moose, Bear and Buck are popular monikers applied to our doggy chums.

Then there are those who simply apply "human" names to their canine companions—Hugh, Eugene, Victor...Joe??!

Big Shots

J.P. Morgan

I've noticed over the years that many important men substitute initials for their given names. J. P. Morgan, E. F. Hutton, J. Edgar Hoover to name a few. I often wonder why and when the conversion was made. Is it determined by income? Age and income? Office location perhaps?

I'm thinking of converting to initials as well. J. F. Campolo Jr...I like that—very classy. Or for a little flare I'll tack on an extra name at the end...J. F. Campolo Jr. COOLIO...for example. As an aspiring rapper, I think it would work, and as a bonus I could hold some book signings in the hood!

Part 5: Philosophy

Too Hot to Handle

For many years Television stations featured a newscaster or two, a sportscaster and a weatherman. The newsies were the top dogs, commanding most of the programming time, usually followed by the sportscaster. The weatherman always came in last because....well....no one really took them too seriously. The weather was what it was. So the weathermen were usually a little quirky; they may have had a costume, a sidekick or some other gimmick to get people to watch.

This is a weatherman

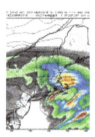

Meteorologist gibberish

That has changed in recent years. These days you have to have a "meteorologist." The meteorologists are less fun—but no more accurate. They have a lot of nifty devices and use impressive terms though. They tell us that's important!

Many networks of late, realizing that people understand the truth about weather forecasts have come to offer a little "fluff" to smooth the hoax over a bit.

Hot, cold, rain, snow...
hurricane...who cares??

Flame War!

I often wonder what The Bard would say were he around today. With current politics and social instability as they are, anger and name calling are at fever pitch. The advent of the Internet—featuring instant information and communication, along with the ability to remain anonymous—has certainly played a roll in the phenomena.

We see an inflammatory news article, Facebook post or Tweet and immediately jump on one side of the camp or the other—shooting flames from our computers and I-phones via social media or Internet comment boards. Shakespeare would probably find the activity as irresistible as the rest of us do, using his keen observatory nature and sharp wit to skewer anyone crossing his path.

Oh cometh thou join the fun, Sir William!

Who?

John Wayne was a great actor, a tremendous film presence and an American institution. His memorabilia, often signed with his name or his moniker "The Duke," is as popular as ever. I wonder how popular all the coffee mugs, holsters, signed photos etc. would be if they were signed with his real name...Marion Morrison.

That's my name, Pilgrim!

*Subdivisions are often named after the wildlife and fauna destroyed to create them.

Part 5: Philosophy

*Rhode Island is not an island.

*Since Columbus thought he landed in China in 1492, why aren't the Indians called Chinese?

*I spent six months with Nguyen Than Hoa before he was killed in the Vietnam War. I never learned how to pronounce his name, nor did he mine. However we understood each other well enough—and I missed him when he was gone. (photo lost)

*If Amerigo Vespucci had been named Roberto Vespucci, we would be called Bobbicans?

Part 5: Philosophy

Gotta love the Grandfolks!

*My paternal grandfather, Demetrius Campolo, was by all accounts, a tough character to live with and an even tougher character to like. He died the year I was born, but over the years, stories of his antics rose to the surface. My grandmother Jenny, his long suffering wife, apparently got some modem of revenge when he passed. She never cared for his given name and always called him Dominic, despite the fact that calling him Dominic brought her additional grief—a commodity which she and her fourteen children already had a surplus of largely thanks to Demetrius. Nevertheless, after the passing of Demetrius, Grandma Jenny had "Dominic Campolo" inscribed on his tombstone...an act of defiance with an immortal flavor.

Well played Grandma!

Demetrius/Dominic Campolo   *Grandma Jenny Campolo*

Houston, We have a Problem...

When I was in Vietnam, the Vietnamese would often point to the name tag on my uniform and make a rocket sound, while pointing their finger toward the sky. The Apollo space program was still in play and they apparently

thought there was enough similarity in Apollo and Campolo to make the connection. Sometimes the Vietnamese were a hoot.

You Slay Me

Quite a few people have been executed for treason over the years. While some have been executed for your standard, garden variety "Treason," others have had the distinction of being executed for "High Treason." If I'm going to be heckled, drawn, quartered and then hung, hey, do me the honor. Give me a "High."

Sir William Wallace

MORE PHILOSOPHY, QUOTES FROM OTHERS

If you share these quotes, please credit the original author.

Go to heaven for the climate and hell for the company.

~Benjamin Franklin Wade

While we wait for life, life passes.

~Seneca

Write it through your own special lenses. Write it because it won't go away until you do…

~Joyce Faulkner

Patriotism in its simplest, clearest, and most indubitable meaning is nothing but an instrument for the attainment of the government's ambitious and mercenary aims, and a renunciation of human dignity, common sense, and conscience by the governed, and a slavish submission to those who hold power. That is what is really preached wherever patriotism is championed. Patriotism is slavery.

~Leo Tolstoy

Patriotism is the last refuge of the scoundrel.

~ Samuel Johnson

Bolshevism is knocking at our gates, we can't afford to let it in... We must keep America whole and safe and unspoiled. We must keep the worker away from red literature and red ruses; we must see that his mind remains healthy.

~Al Capone

I'm a kind person, I'm kind to everyone, but if you are unkind to me, then kindness is not what you'll remember me for.

~Capone

The donkey may travel to Mecca, but it's still an ass.

~Arabian proverb

If you have any young friends who aspire to become writers, the second-greatest favor you can do them is to present them with copies of *The Elements of Style*. The first-greatest, of course, is to shoot them now, while they're happy.

~Dorothy Parker

What is life? It is the flash of a firefly in the night. It is the breath of a buffalo in the wintertime. It is the little shadow which runs across the grass and loses itself in the sunset.

~Crowfoot, Blackfoot warrior

Part 5: More Philosophy, Quotes from Others

An object in possession seldom retains the same charm that it had in pursuit.

~Pliny the Elder

My brother need not be idealized, or enlarged in death beyond what he was in life; to be remembered simply as a good and decent man, who saw wrong and tried to right it, saw suffering and tried to heal it, saw war and tried to stop it.

~Ted Kennedy, eulogy for his brother Bobby Kennedy

The best time to plant a tree was twenty years ago, the second best time is today.

~Chinese proverb

Do not go to the camps, nothing comes out of the camps. Nothing.

~From Lena Olin's character, Rose Mather, speaking on the WWII concentration camps in the 2008 film "The Reader"

I'm a writer. I use people for what I write. Let the world beware.

~Catherine Tramell (Sharon Stone), Basic Instinct

I shall be an autocrat, that's my trade. And the Lord will forgive me, that's his.

~Catherine the Great

Part 5: More Philosophy, Quotes from Others

Make your money, then form your ethics.

~Observation by Bill Van Lone, an early mentor to Joe

*Spiro Agnew, one of many wealthy American's crooks who got caught with their hand in the cookie jar...and got a way with it.

In the land of the blind, the one eyed man is king.

~Desiderius Erasmus

The sun, with all those planets revolving around it and dependent on it, can still ripen a bunch of grapes as if it had nothing else in the universe to do.

~Galileo Galilei

Do not mistake covert operations for missionary work.

~Henry Kissinger

There are three rules for writing a novel. Unfortunately no one knows what they are.

~ W. Somerset Maugham

I am accustomed to sleep and in my dreams to imagine the same things that lunatics imagine when awake.

~Descartes

At times while awake, I imagine what lunatics must muse during their sleep.

~Joe

Lettin' the cat outta the bag is a whole lot easier 'n puttin' it back in.

~Will Rogers

Lies are the religion of slaves and masters. Truth is the god of the free man.

~Maxim Gorky

And what does anyone know about traitors, or why Judas did what he did?

~Jean Rhys

The contents of his pockets were often emptied into the hands of small, ragged little boys, nor could he understand how so much wealth should go brushing by, unmindful of the poor.

~Annie Oakley, speaking on Sitting Bull

A happy ending depends on where you end your story.

~Orson Welles

A person hears only what they understand.

~Johann Wolfgang

Give neither counsel nor salt, until you are asked for it.

~Italian proverb

Part 5: More Philosophy, Quotes from Others

I live for nights that I can't remember, with people that I won't forget.

~Drake

> I on the other hand, live for nights that I can't forget with people that I won't remember.
>
> ~Joe

Young men, hear an old man to whom old men hearkened when he was young.

~ Gaius Octavius Thurinus (Augustus)

> (Yeah... what Auggie said)

The Cisco Kid was a friend of mine. The Cisco Kid was a friend of mine. He drink whiskey Poncho drink the wine. He drink whiskey Poncho drink the wine. We met down on the fort of Rio Grande. We met down on the fort of Rio Grande.

~ '70s Rock group: War

Remember, you are just an extra in everyone else's play.

~Franklin Roosevelt

In politics, stupidity is not a handicap.

~Napoleon Bonaparte

> (This is proven every day on Internet posts and Facebook)

Part 5: More Philosophy, Quotes from Others

Now here's what I'm gonna do!

That's bullshit. You're not gonna do nothin' like that. I'll tell you what you gonna do. You gonna get a job. That's what you gonna do. You're gonna get a little job. Some job a convict can get, like scraping off trays in a cafeteria. Or cleaning out toilets. And you're gonna hold onto that job like gold. Because it is gold. Let me tell you, Jack, that is gold. You listenin' to me? And when that man walks in at the end of the day. And he comes to see how you done, you ain't gonna look in his eyes. You gonna look at the floor. Because you don't want to see that fear in his eyes when you jump up & grab his face, and slam him to the floor, and make him scream & cry for his life. So you look right at the floor, Jack. Pay attention to what I'm sayin', motherfucker! And then he's gonna look around the room—see how you done. And he's gonna say "Oh, you missed a little spot over there. Jeez, you didn't get this one here. What about this little bitty spot?" And you're gonna suck all that pain inside you, and you're gonna clean that spot. And you're gonna clean that spot. Until you get that shiny clean. And on Friday, you pick up your paycheck. And if you could do that, if you could do that, you could be president of Chase Manhattan... corporations! If you could do that.

~Oscar "Manny" Manheim, Runaway Train

(OK, damn Manny!)

I have noticed that even those who assert that everything is predestined and that we can change nothing about it still look both ways before they cross the street.

~Stephen Hawking

You can't put shit back into the donkey.

~Tony Soprano

Part 5: More Philosophy, Quotes from Others

We cannot solve our problems with the same thinking we used when we created them.

~Albert Einstein

This isn't Nam...there are rules here.

~Walter Sobchak, The Big Lebowski

Home is the place where, when you go there, they have to take you in.

~Robert Frost

The measure of who we are is what we do with what we have.

~Vince Lombardi

A man who chases two rabbits catches neither.

~Chinese proverb

The knowledge of yourself will preserve you from vanity.

~Miguel de Cervantes

Part 5: More Philosophy, Quotes from Others

Nothing strengthens authority so much as silence.

~Leonardo da Vinci

A mule will labor ten years willingly and patiently for you, just for the privilege of kicking you once.

~William Faulkner

Men marry because they are tired; women, because they are curious; both are disappointed.

~Oscar Wilde

But how could one live and have no story to tell

~Fyodor Doestoevsky

Military justice is to justice what military music is to music.

~Groucho Marx

"Yes, very sensible… People die of common sense, Dorian, one lost moment at a time. Life is a moment. There is no hereafter. So make it burn always with the hardest flame."

~Oscar Wilde; The Picture of Dorian Gray

"Live! Live the wonderful life that is in you! Let nothing be lost upon you. Be always searching for new sensations. Be afraid of nothing."

~Wilde

Part 5: More Philosophy, Quotes from Others

First prize is a Cadillac, second prize is a set of steak knives… third prize is your fired.

~Glen Gary Glenn Ross

Indeed, history is nothing more than a tableau of crimes and misfortunes.

~Voltaire

It is forbidden to kill; therefore all murderers are punished unless they kill in large numbers and to the sound of trumpets.

~Voltaire

A man cannot be comfortable without his own approval.

~Mark Twain

The man who doesn't read good books has no advantage over the man who can't read them.

~Twain

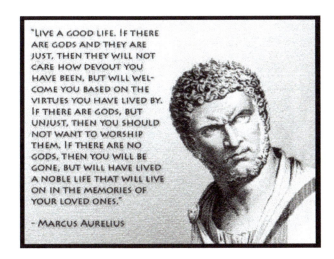

If you have a garden and a library, you have everything you need.

~Marcus Tullius Cicero

The sinews of war are infinite money.

~Cicero

Every gun that is made, every warship launched, every rocket fired signifies in the final sense, a theft from those who hunger and are not fed, those who are cold and are not clothed. This world in arms is not spending money alone. It is spending the sweat of its laborers, the genius of its scientists, the hopes of its children. This is not a way of life at all in any true sense. Under the clouds of war, it is humanity hanging on a cross of iron.

~Dwight D. Eisenhower

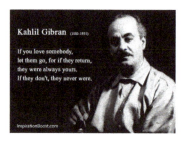

A fox looked at his shadow at sunrise and said, "I will have a camel for lunch today." And all morning he went about looking for camels. But at noon he saw his shadow again—and he said, "A mouse will do."

~Gibran

If a politician found he had cannibals among his constituents he would promise them missionaries for dinner.

~H.L. Mencken

Anyone who has ever taken a shower has had a great idea.

~Nolan Bushnell

Part 5: More Philosophy, Quotes from Others

The vulgar crowd always is taken by appearances, and the world consists chiefly of the vulgar.

~Niccolo Machiavelli

When logic and proportion
Have fallen slowly dead
And the White Knight is talking backwards
And the Red Queen's off with her head
Remember what the dormouse said
"Feed your head, feed your head"

~Gracie Slick, White Rabbit

*Joe's note—this song made infinite sense to us in Vietnam

I think now, looking back, we did not fight the enemy; we fought ourselves. And the enemy was in us. The war is over for me now, but it will always be there, the rest of my days. As I'm sure Elias will be, fighting with Barnes for what Rhah called possession of my soul. There are times since, I've felt like the child born of those two fathers. But, be that as it may, those of us who did make it have an obligation to build again, to teach to others what we know, and to try with what's left of our lives to find a goodness and a meaning to this life.

~Taylor; Platoon

I cook with wine; sometimes I even add it to the food.

~W.C. Fields

My psychiatrist told me I was crazy so I told him I wanted a second opinion. He said okay, you're ugly too.

~Rodney Dangerfield

If you cannot bite, do not show your teeth.

~Vietnamese saying

Truth never damages a cause that is just.

~Mahatma Gandhi

The past is something that's already happened and can never be changed. At some point, you have to give up whatever resentment you have towards people, circumstances, and experiences from your past. Otherwise, your future starts to look an awful lot like your past.

~Srinivas Rao

Fairy tales are true: not because they tell us that dragons exist, but because they tell us that dragons can be beaten.

~Neil Gaiman

If I did not write to empty my mind, I would go mad.

~Lord Byron

Part 5: More Philosophy, Quotes from Others

We are stardust
Billion year old carbon
We are golden
Caught in the devil's bargain
And we've got to get ourselves
back to the garden.

Woodstock

~Joni Mitchell

The World breaks everyone, and afterward, some are strong at the broken places.

~Ernest Hemingway

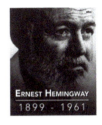

You don't get to choose how you're going to die. Or when. You can decide how you're going to live though.

~Joan Baez

We know what memories can bring; they bring diamonds and rust.

~Baez

I used to be known as a bullshitter but that didn't pay anything. I began calling myself a storyteller – a little better, more prestige – but it still didn't pay anything. I became a freelance writer. At first it was more free than lance, then I finally started getting money for my words.

~Chibenashi (Jim Northrup)

Hell is empty...all the devils are here.

-*Shakespeare*

And those who were seen dancing were thought to be insane by those who could not hear the music.

-Friederich Nietzsche

After coming into contact with a religious man, I always feel the need to wash my hands.

-Nietzsche

Men are nearly always willing to believe what they wish.

-Julius Caesar

Before you leave here, Sir, you're going to learn that one of the most brutal things in the world is your average nineteen-year-old American boy.

-*Philip Caputo, A Rumor of War*

On Stage I make love to 25,000 different people, then I go home alone.

~ Janis Joplin

Long you'll live and high you'll fly and smiles you'll give and tears you'll cry and all you'll touch and all you'll see is all your life will ever be.

~Pink Floyd

Closing

This was an enjoyable book to put together and we hope everyone enjoyed reading it. We will close the book with Joe's poem, *Sweet Bird of Youth*.

Sweet Bird of Youth

Oh sweet bird of youth, when did you slip away?
When we were young, it was not clear that you might leave one day.
We had such times on your great wings those days indeed did fly.
And now you're gone we can't recall just when you passed us by.
On those strong wings, how we did soar with strength, fine looks and pluck.
They teased with hope, they offered wealth and they offered luck.
Now as we pine the hours, musing on our loss,
We grasp at straws to find that strength, that health, that vibrant gloss.
While moving on without you, brings us to tear,
Knowing you will not return......leaves us in fear.
Oh, please return, old friend of youth,
Without you now we face the truth.
In time like you we'll slip away,
Our time here gone, with dreams of yesterday.

Dedicated to some friends who have gone before us:

Jim Booth, Don Booth, Bruce Brehm, Dennis Sadowski, Mike Bjorn, Jim Ostlund,- Joe Doksus

JOE CAMPOLO, JR.

Joe Campolo, Jr. is an award winning author, poet and public speaker. A Vietnam War Veteran, Joe writes and speaks about the war, and is a Veteran's advocate. Some of Joe's stories are gripping, some humorous. Joe also writes about other experiences, many of which are also humorous. Joe enjoys fishing, traveling, writing and spending time with his family. Joe loves to hear from his readers.

Putting this book together was a very enjoyable experience. I am indebted to all of the contributors who took the time and effort to provide these writings.

Joe

Authorization to use artwork granted by:

Trieu Hai Hoang

Authorization to use written material granted by:

Joseph Galloway

JoAnn Forrester

Art Reagan

Joyce Faulkner

Philip Caputo

Ric Hunter

Jimmy Fox

Erik Villard

John Podlaski

Kathleen Rodgers

Charles Vinroot

Dwight Zimmerman

Penni Evans

Duke Barrett

Norm Kober

George Dooley

Rick Wehler

Steve Tindall

Gary Labanow

Jimmy Fox

Dick Evenson